Birds and Flowers Coloring Book For Adults

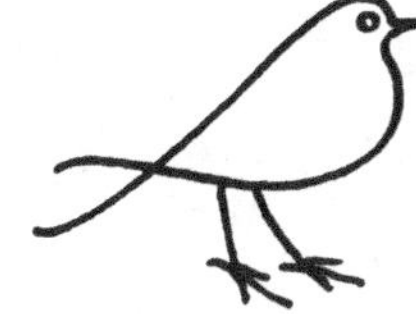

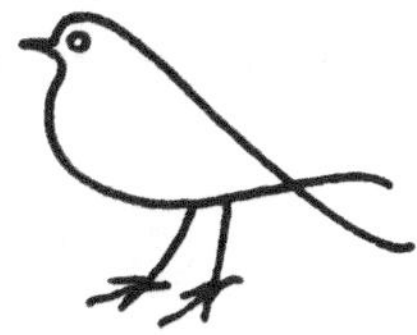

This book belongs to:

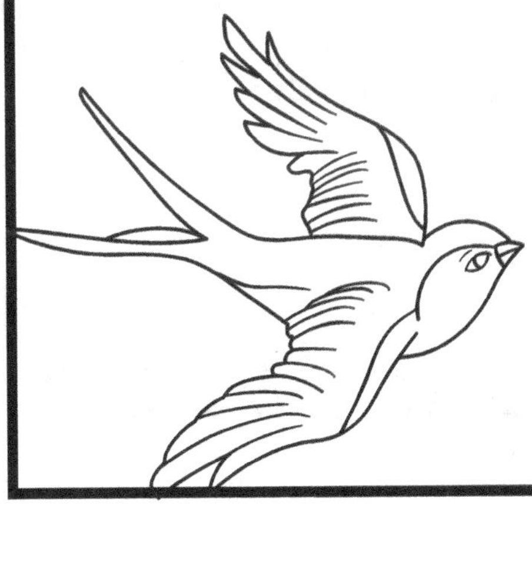

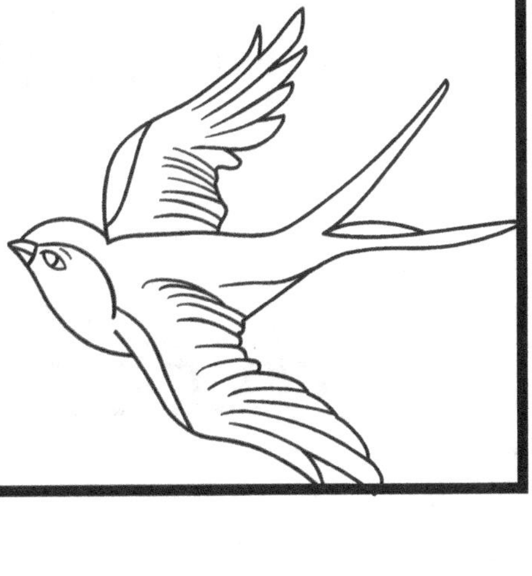

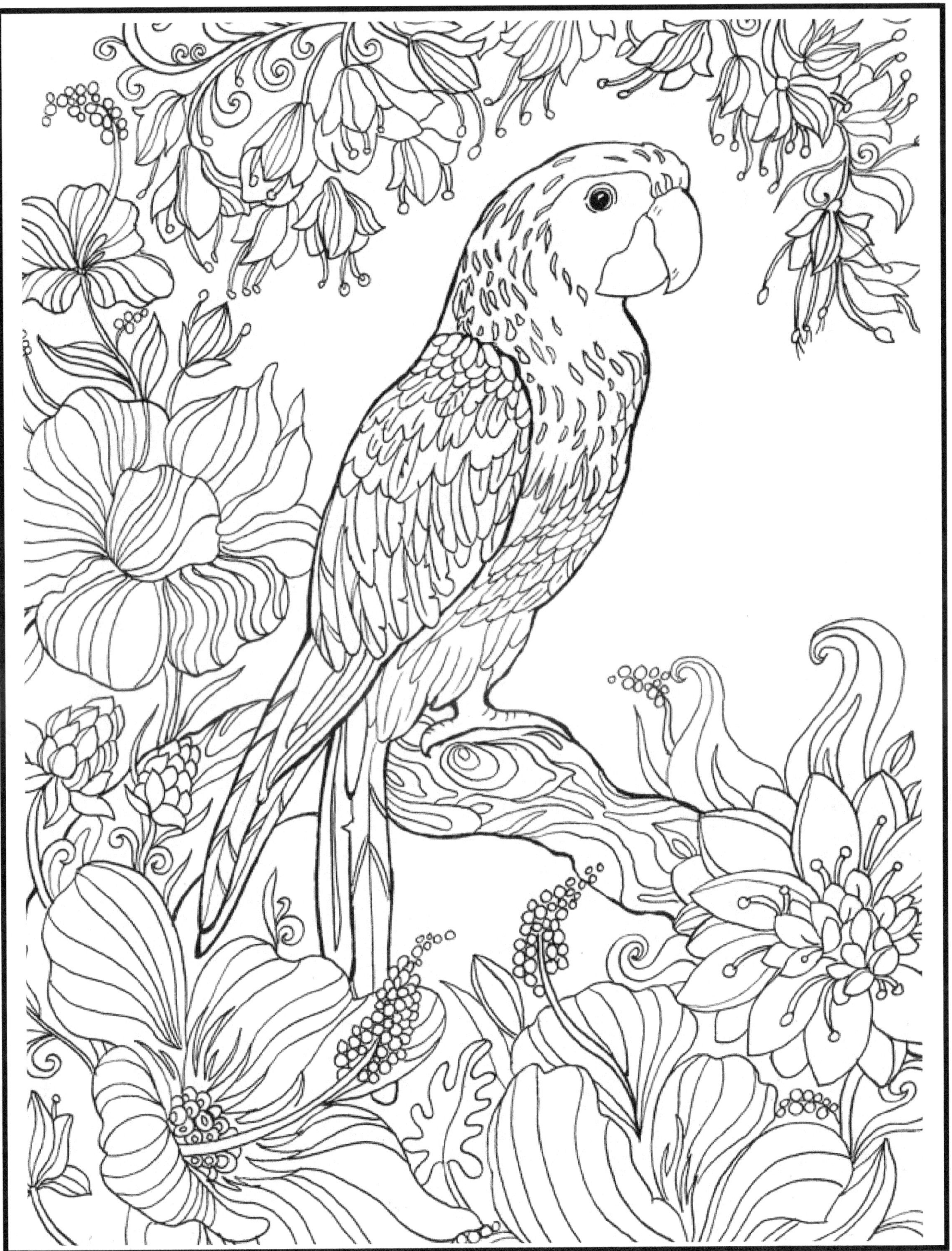

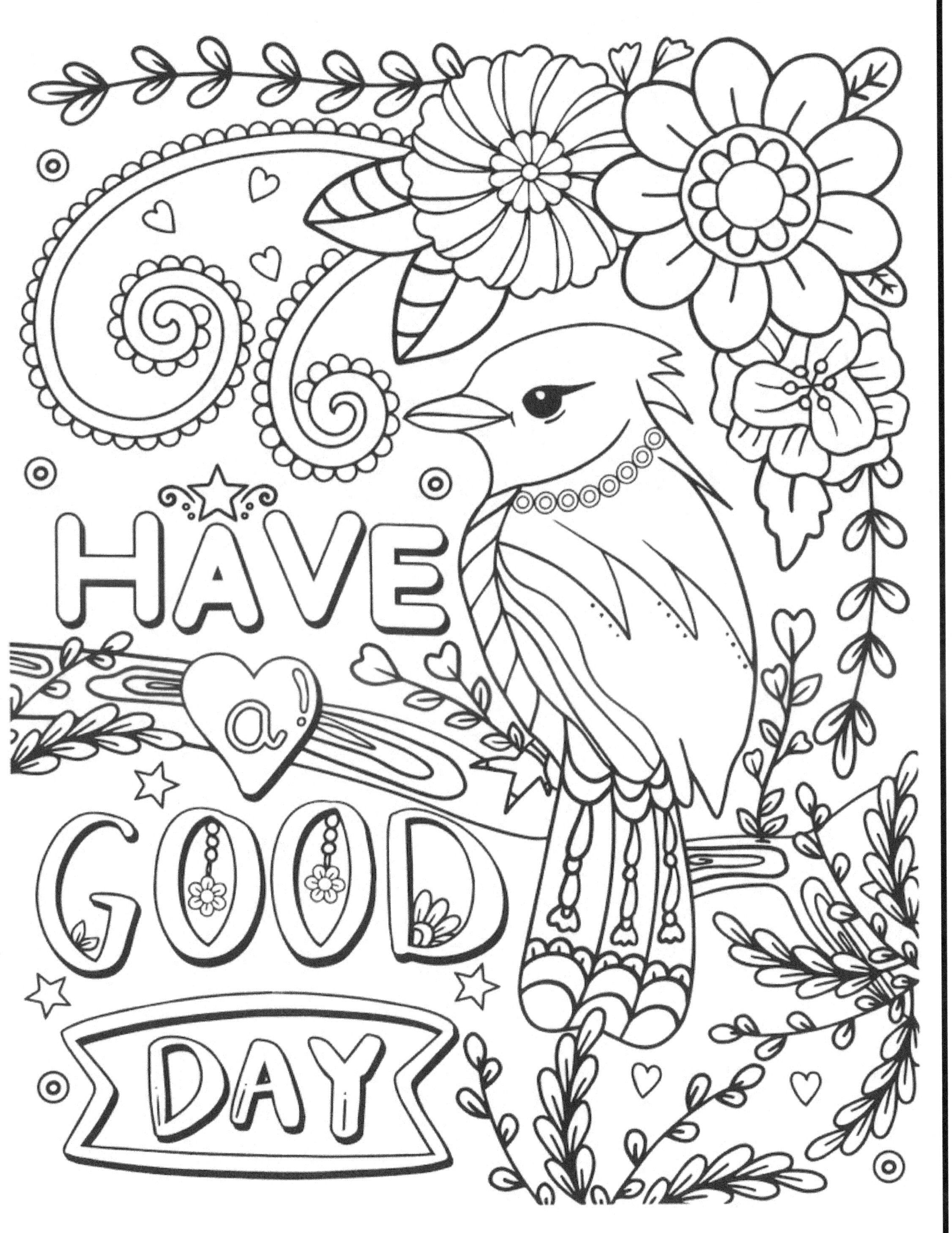

HAVE
a!
GOOD
DAY

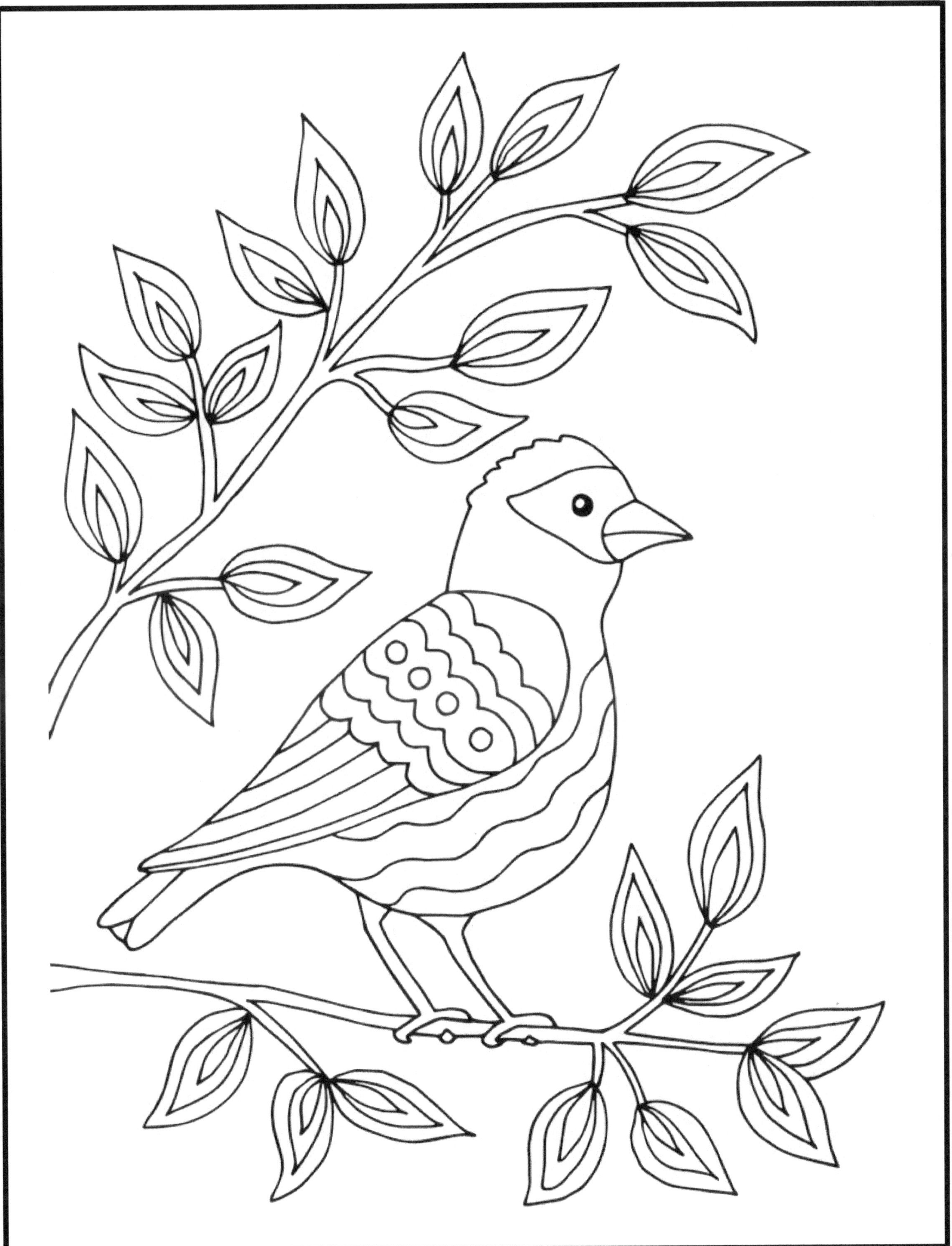

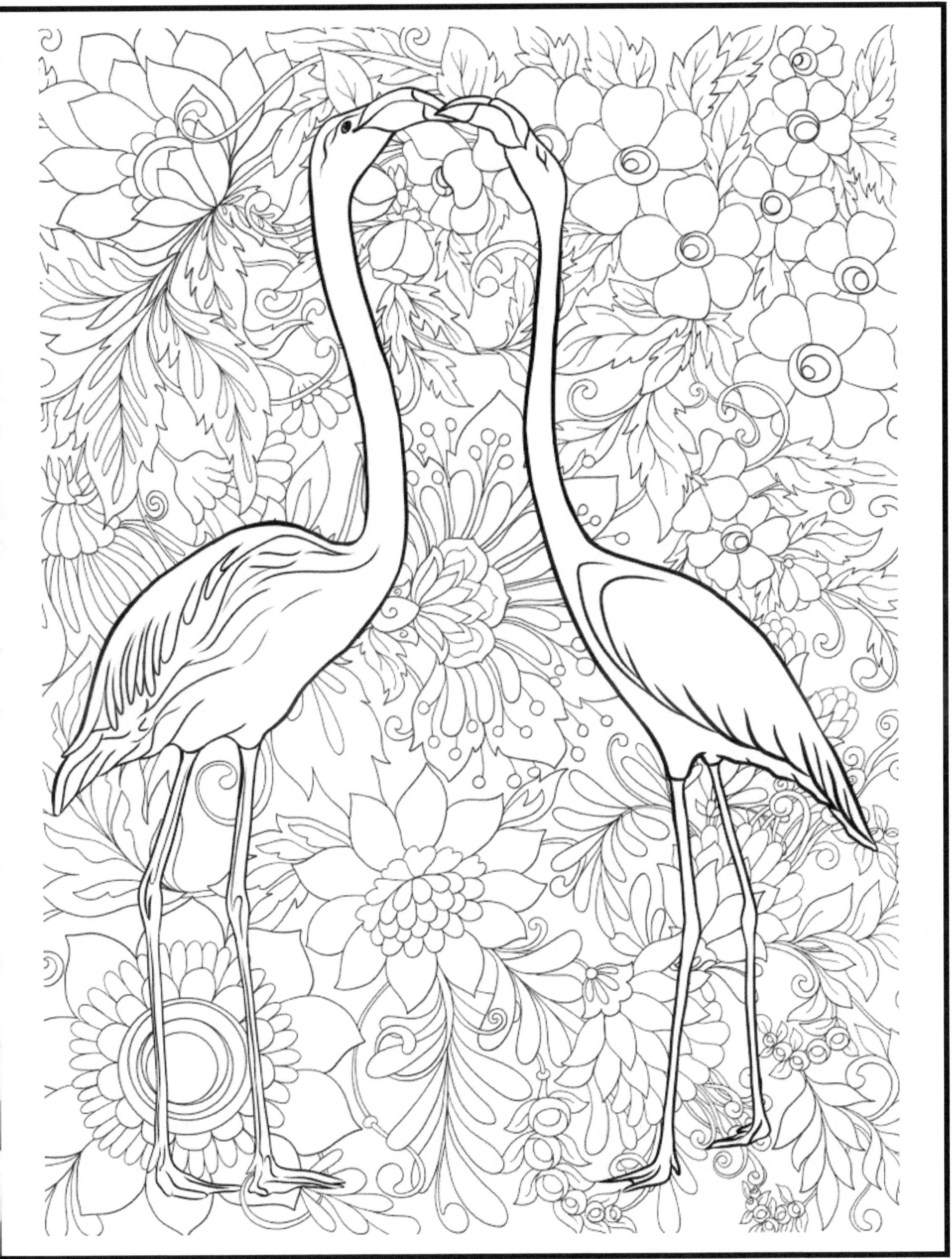

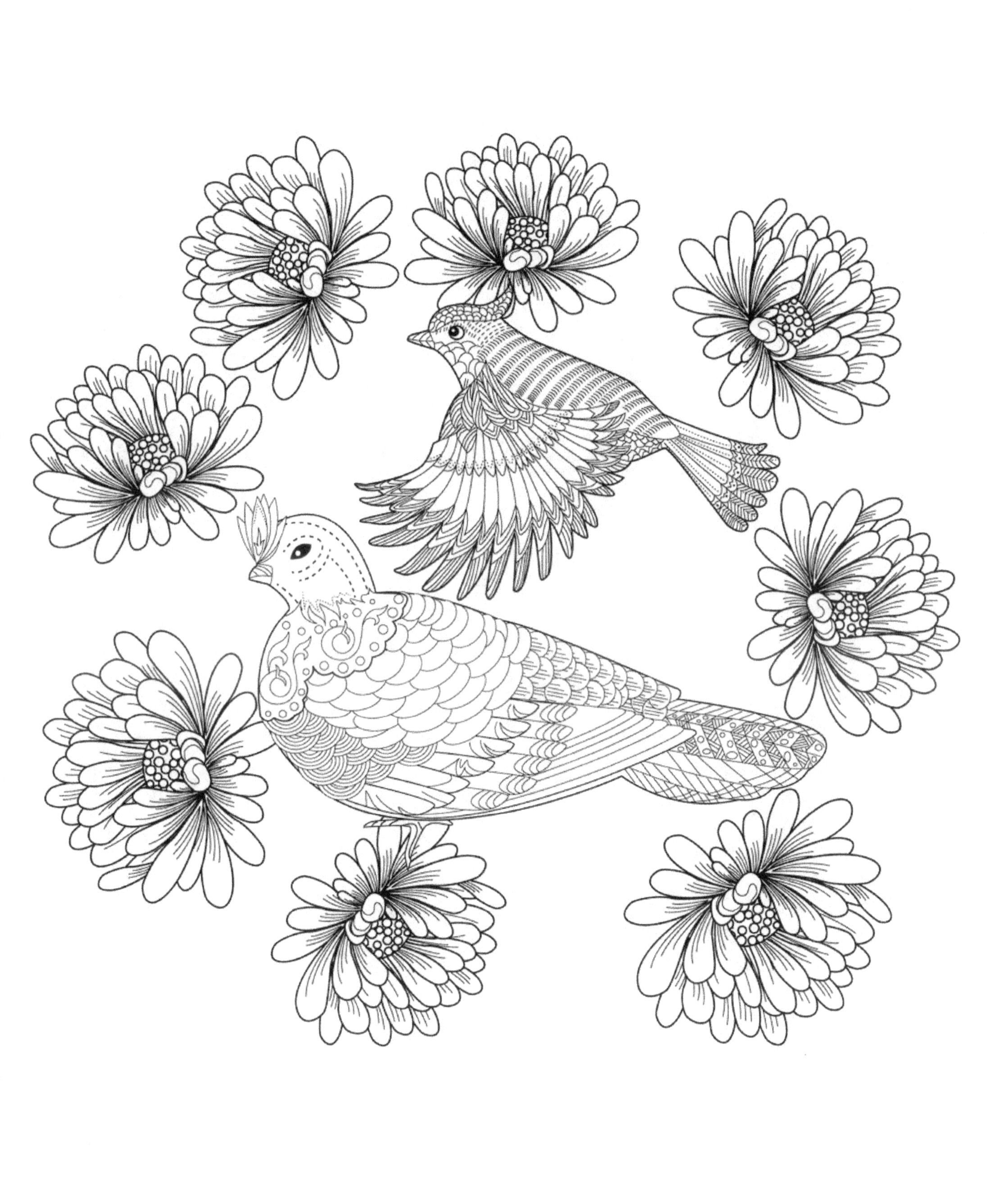

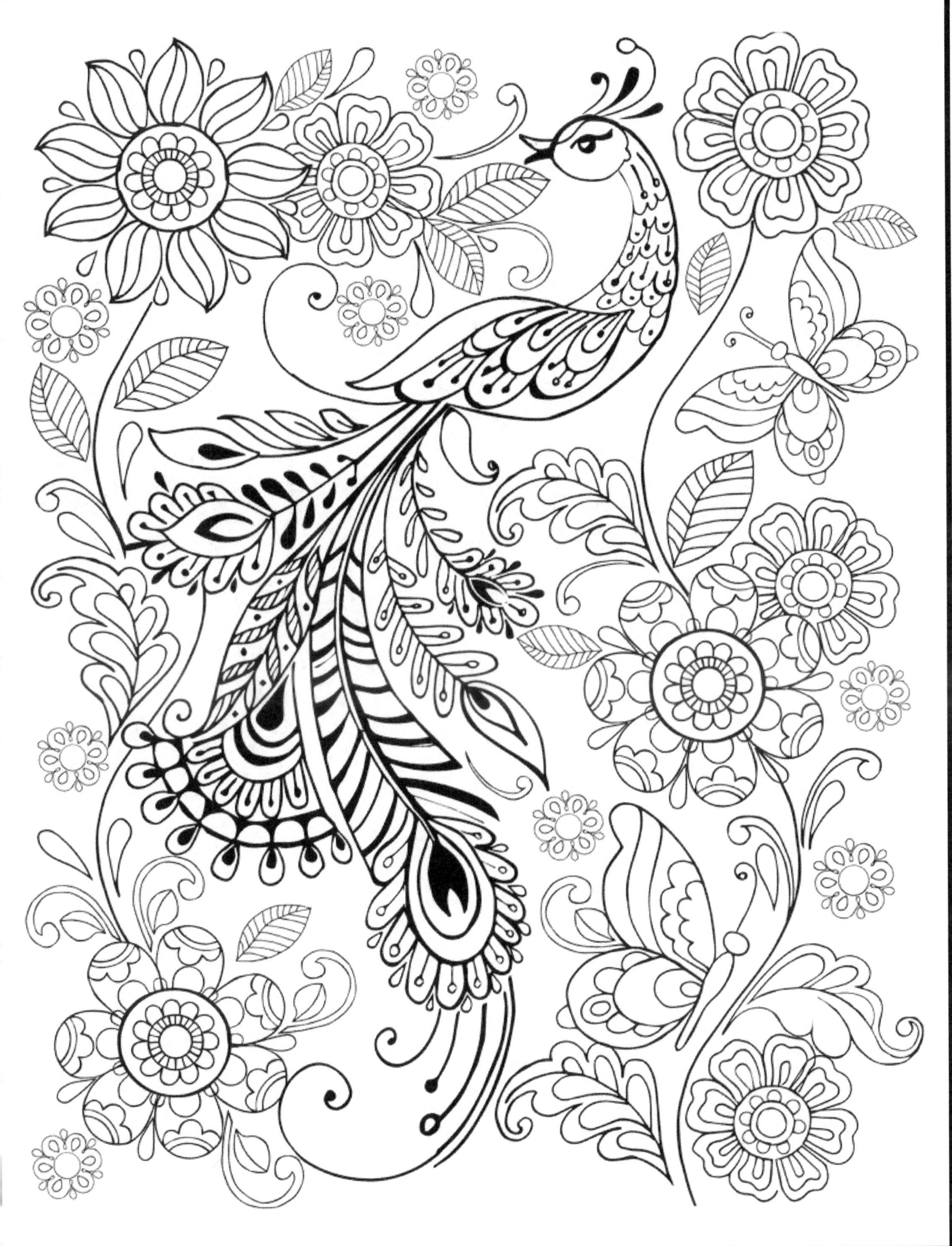

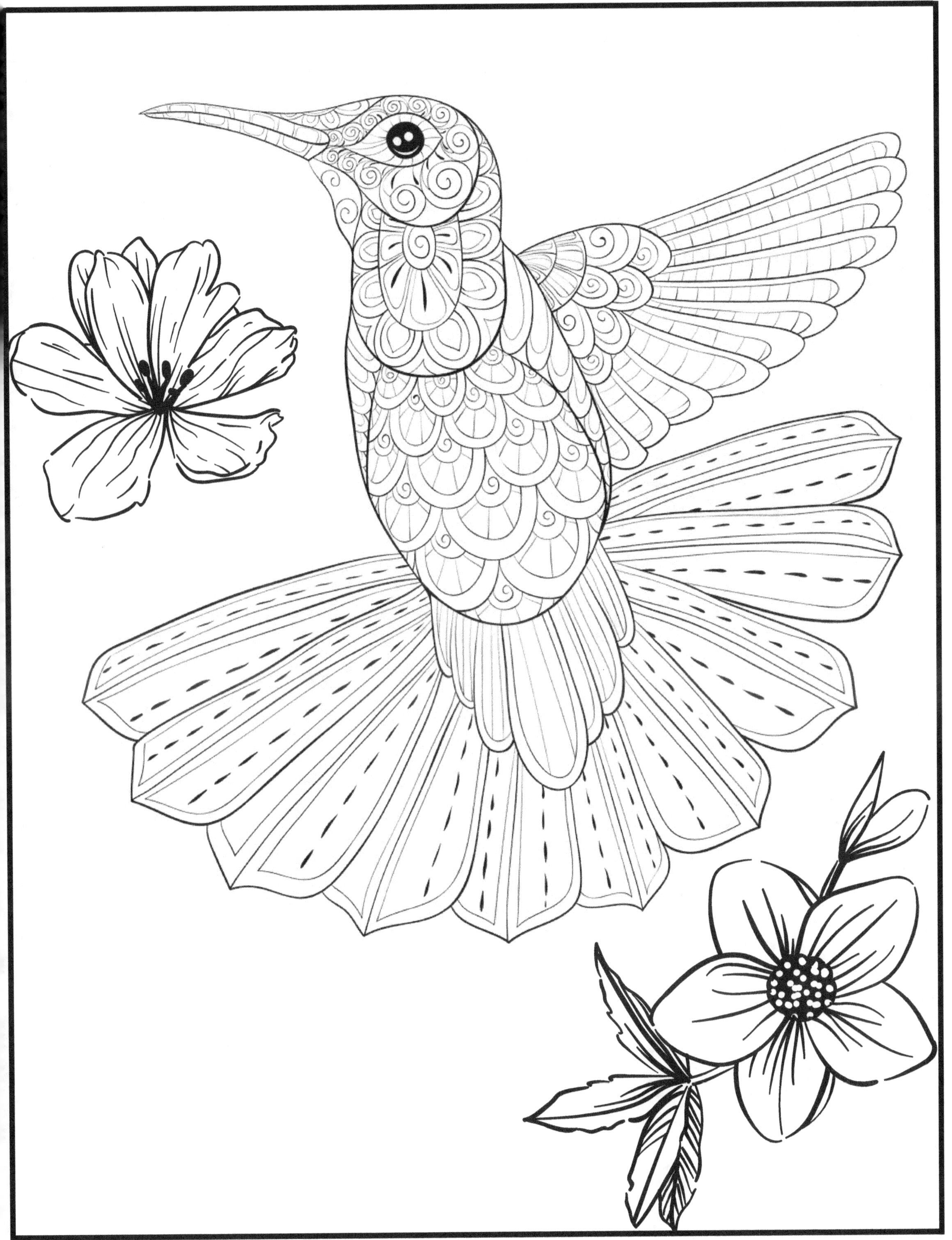

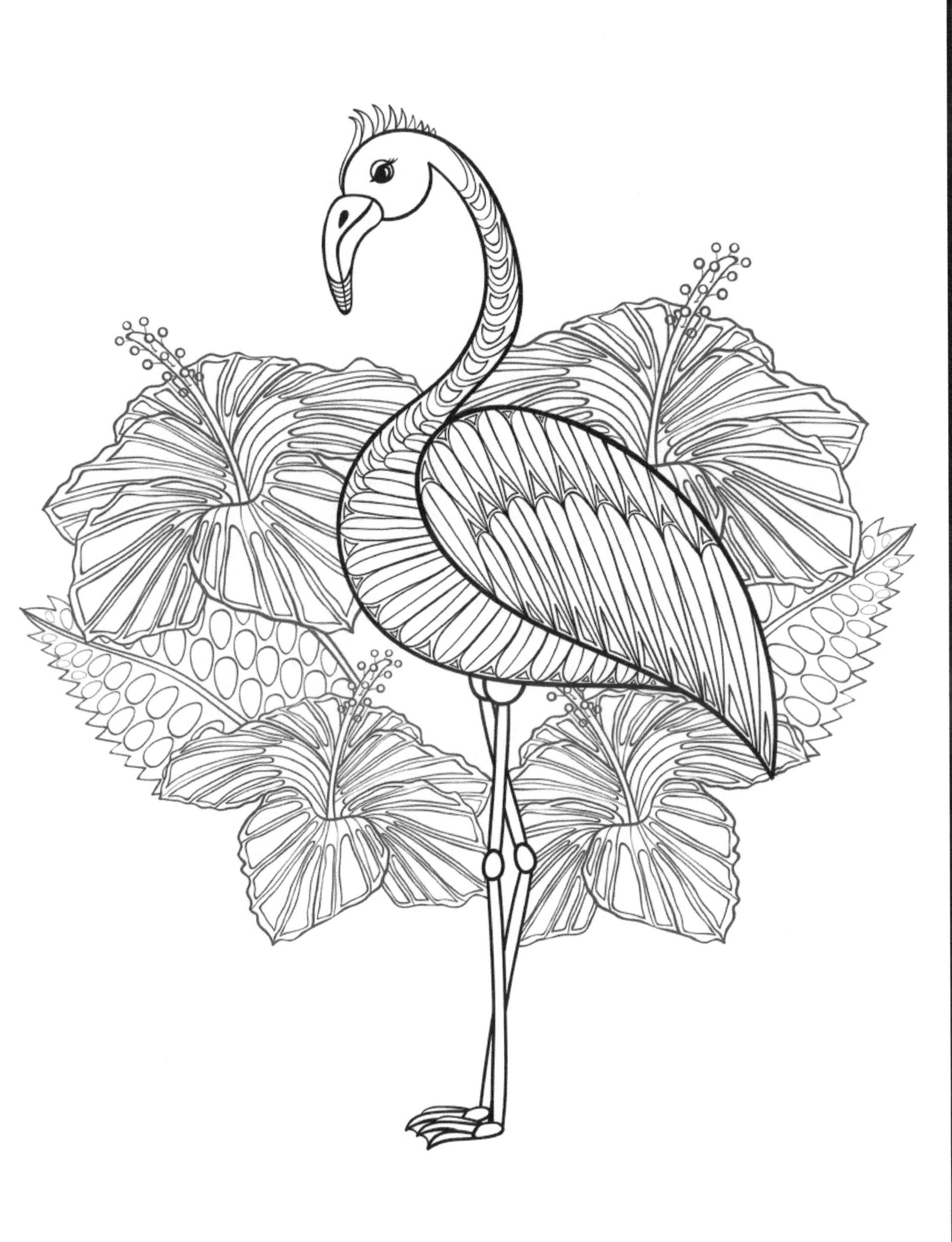

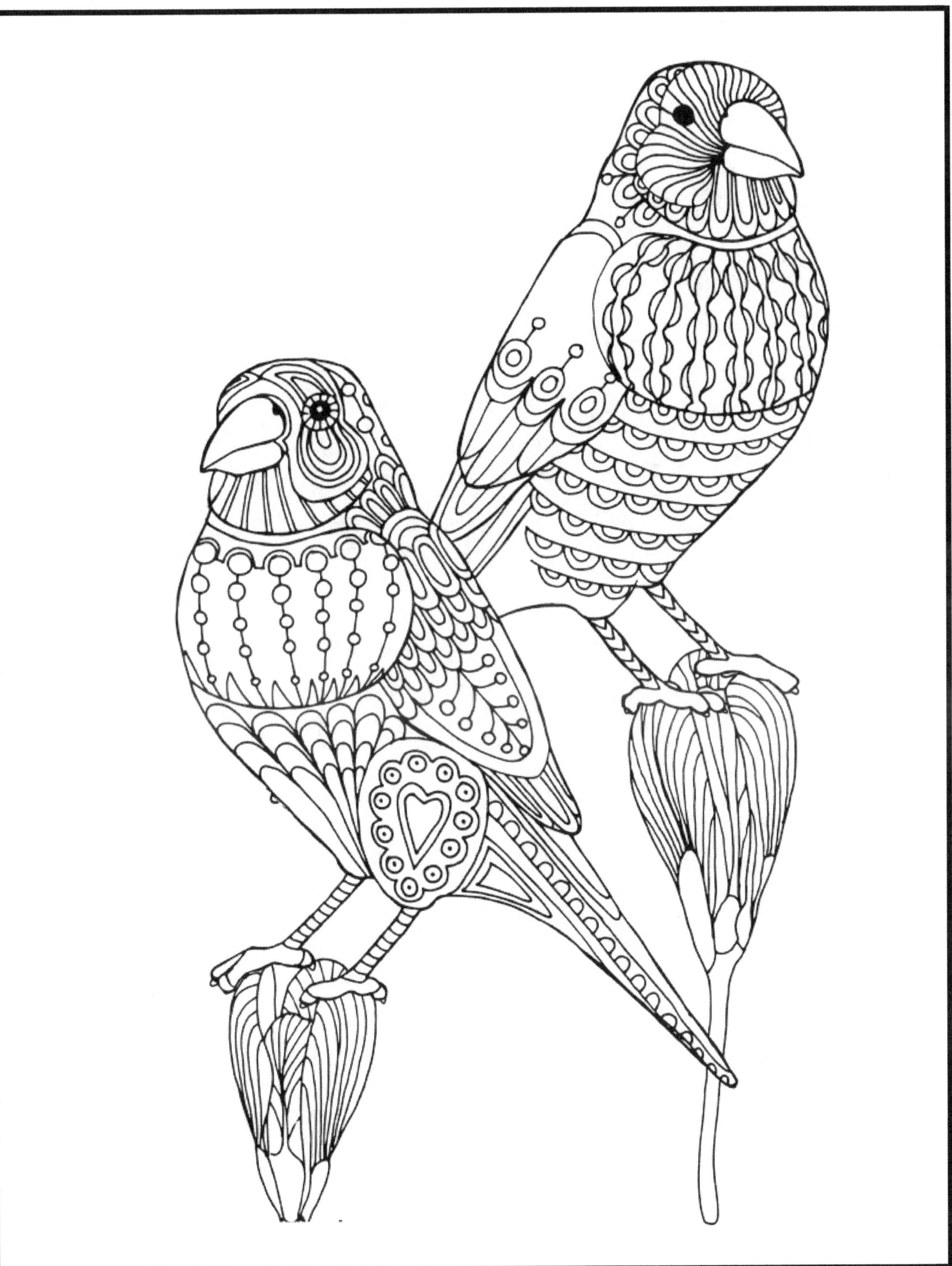

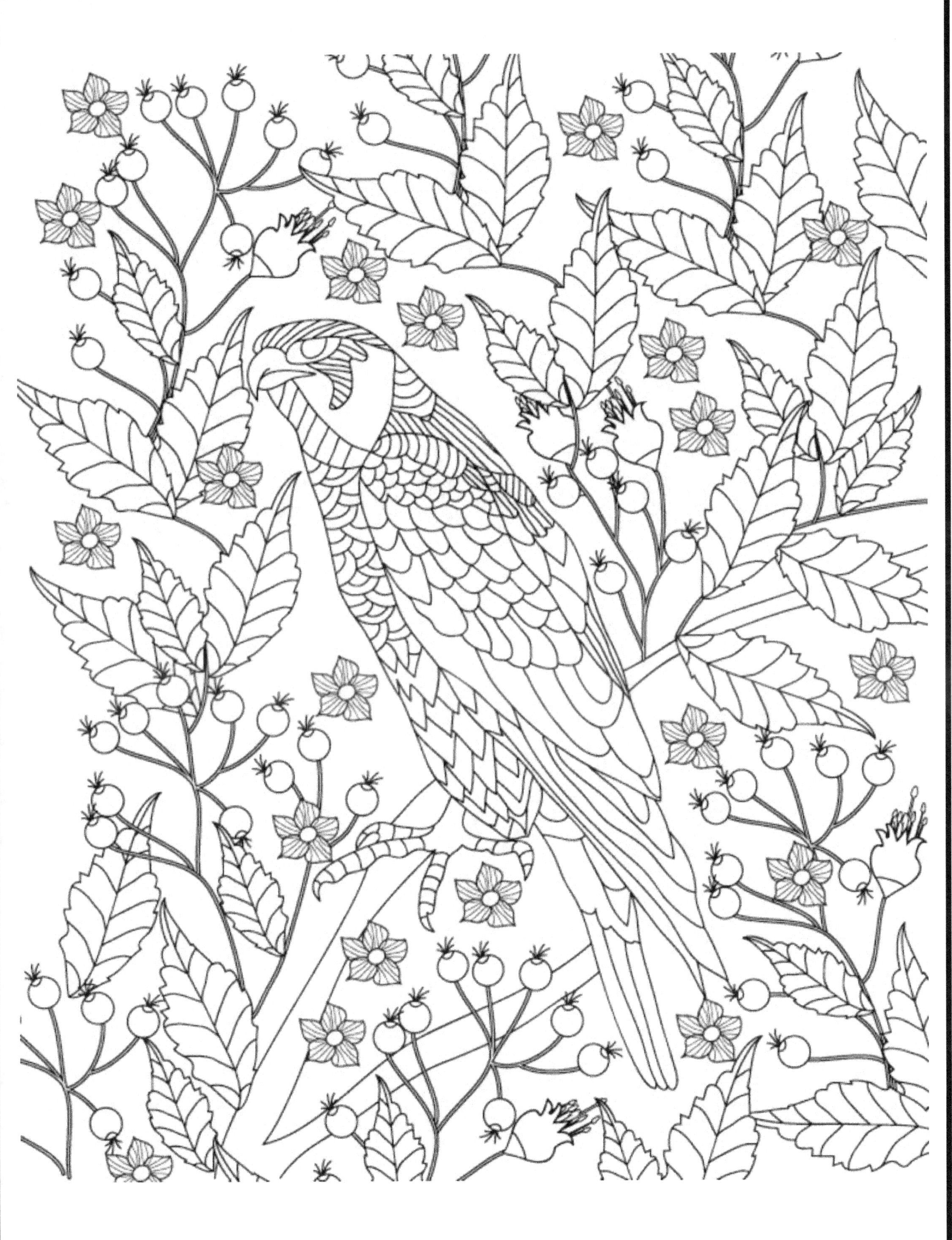

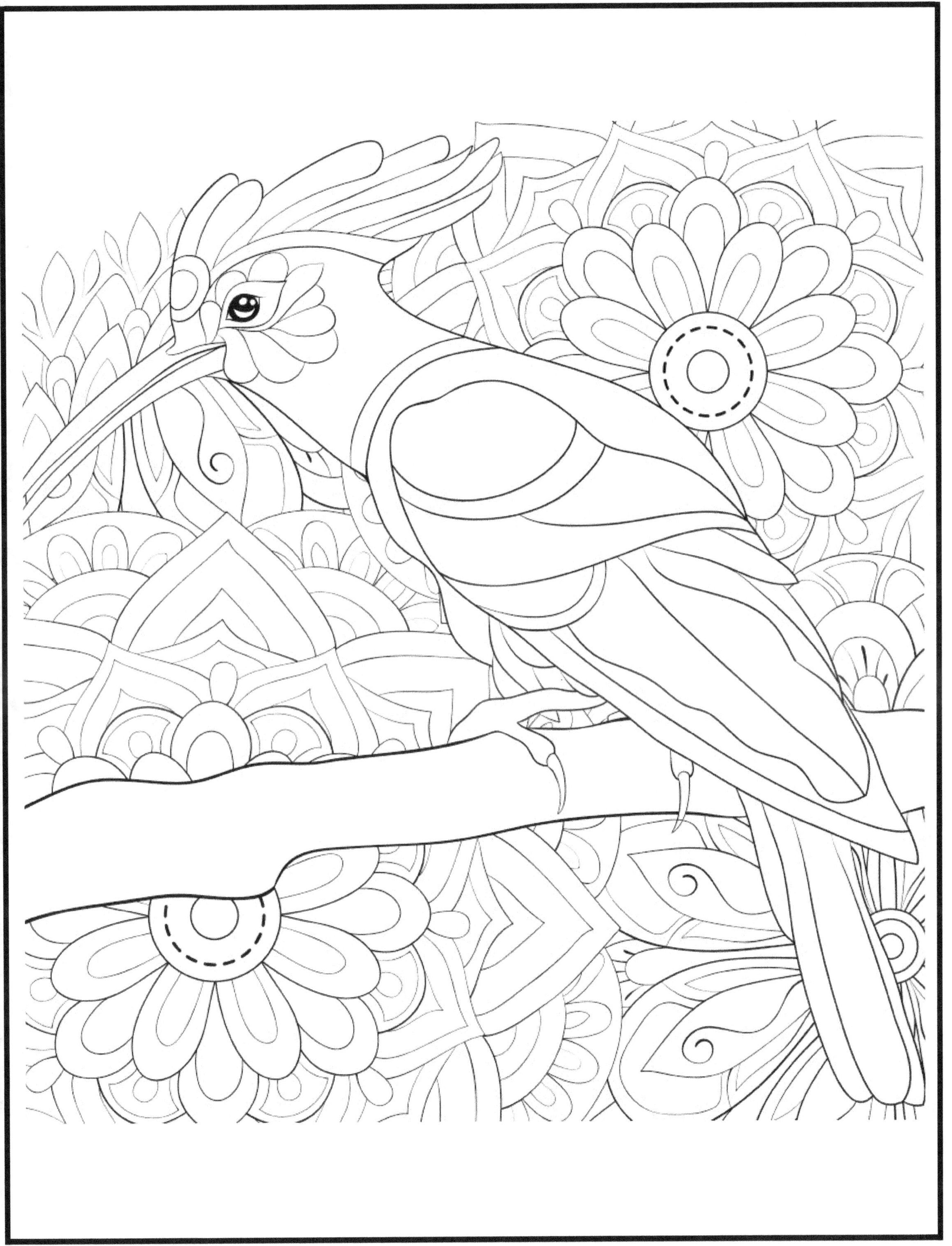

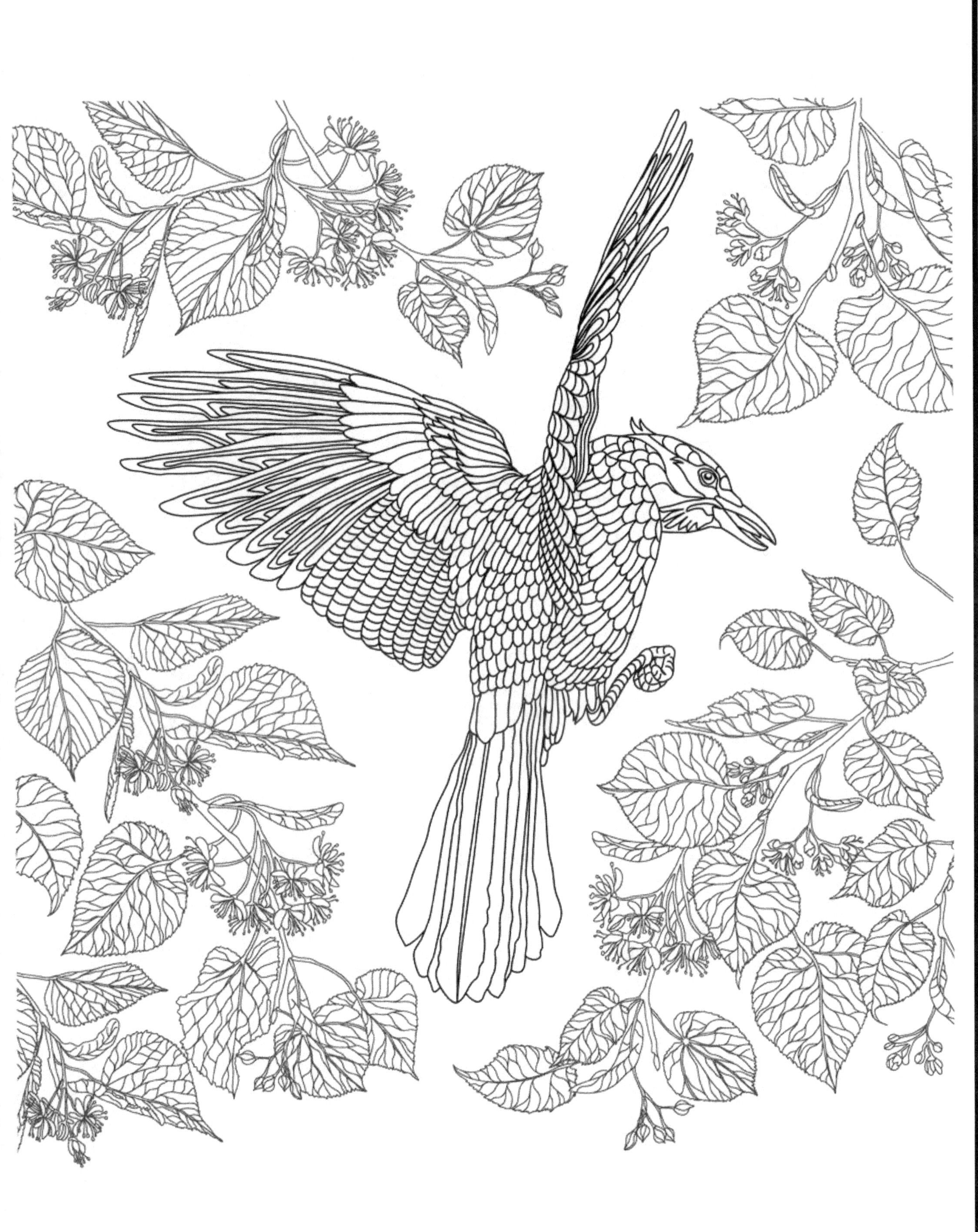

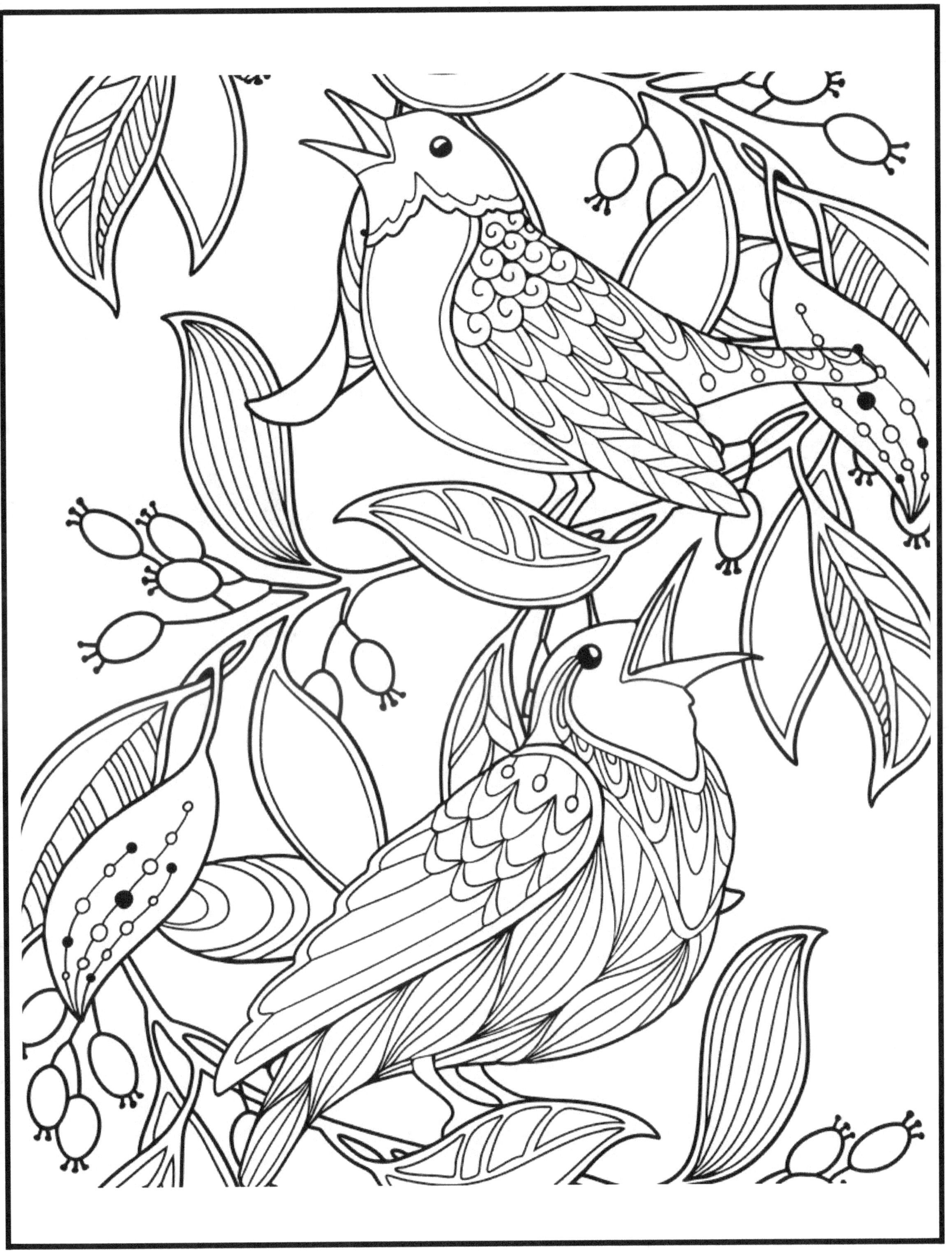

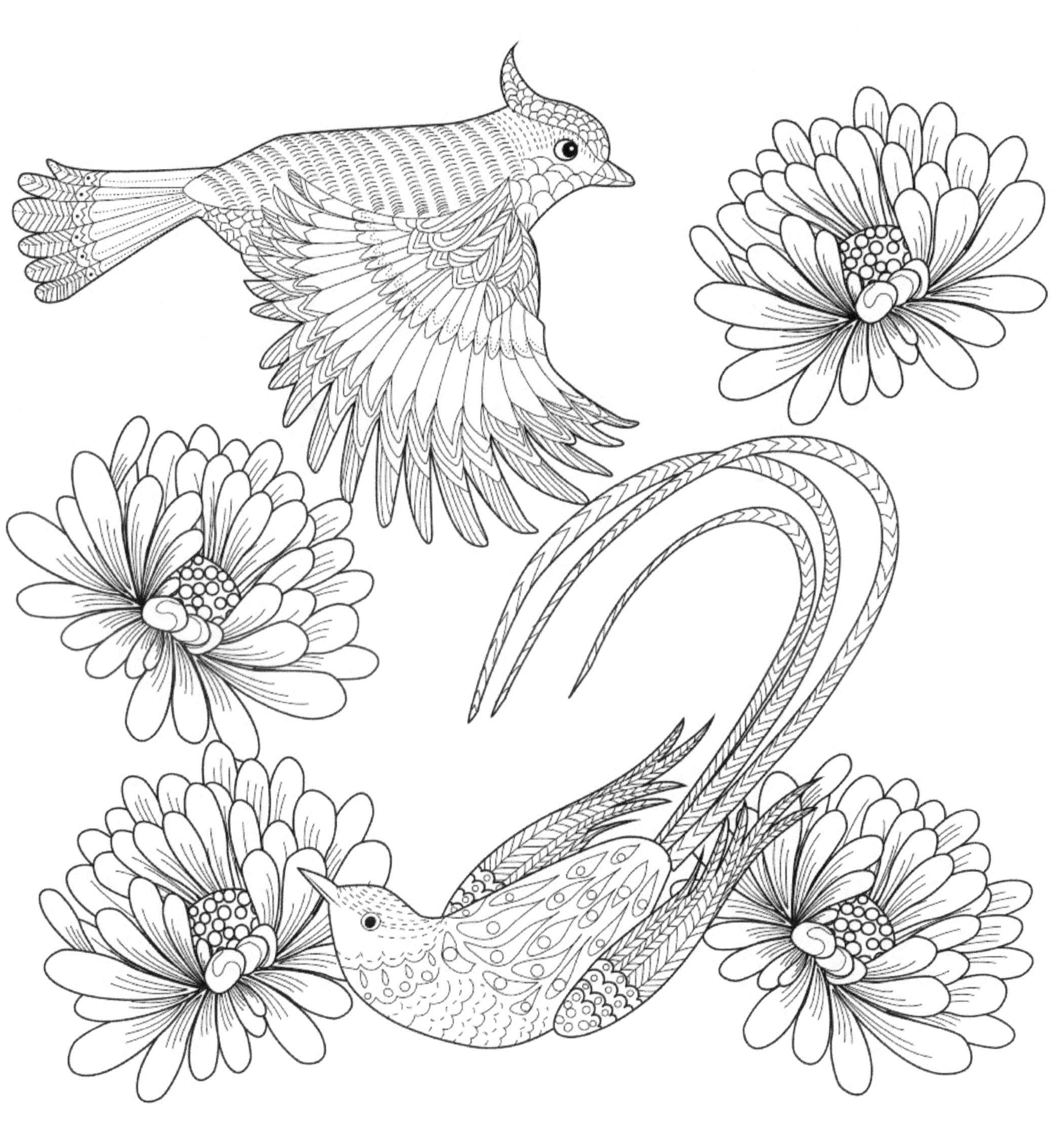

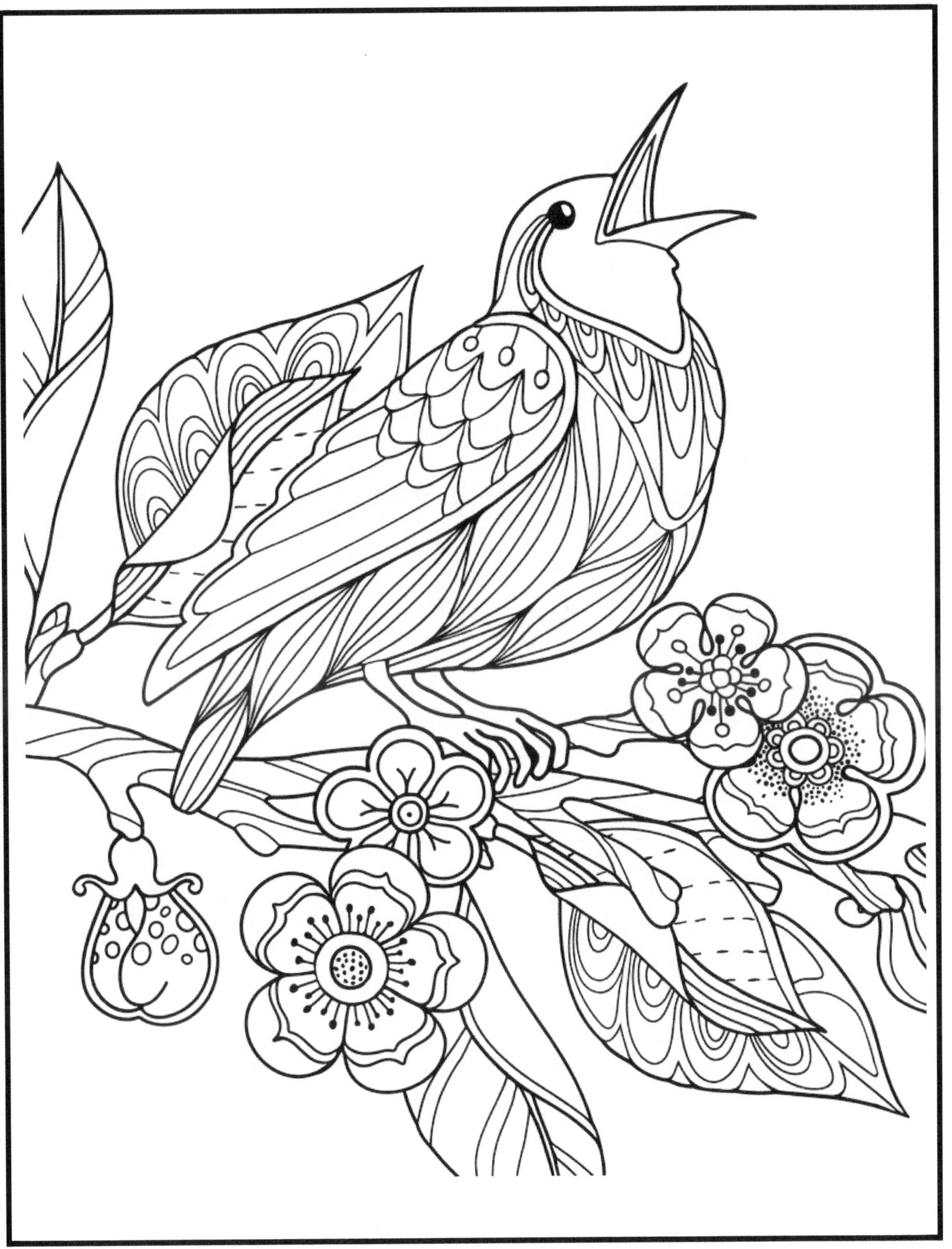

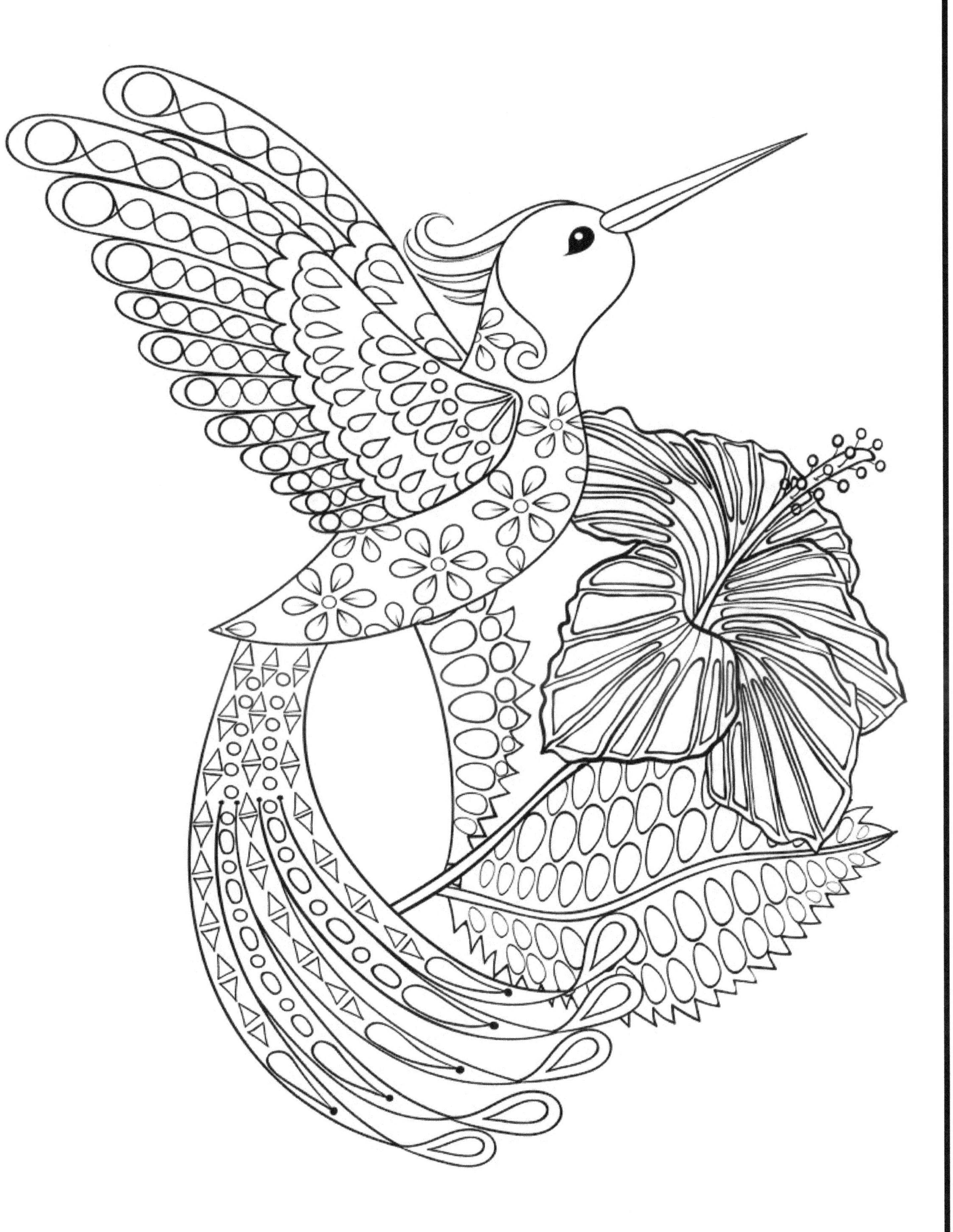

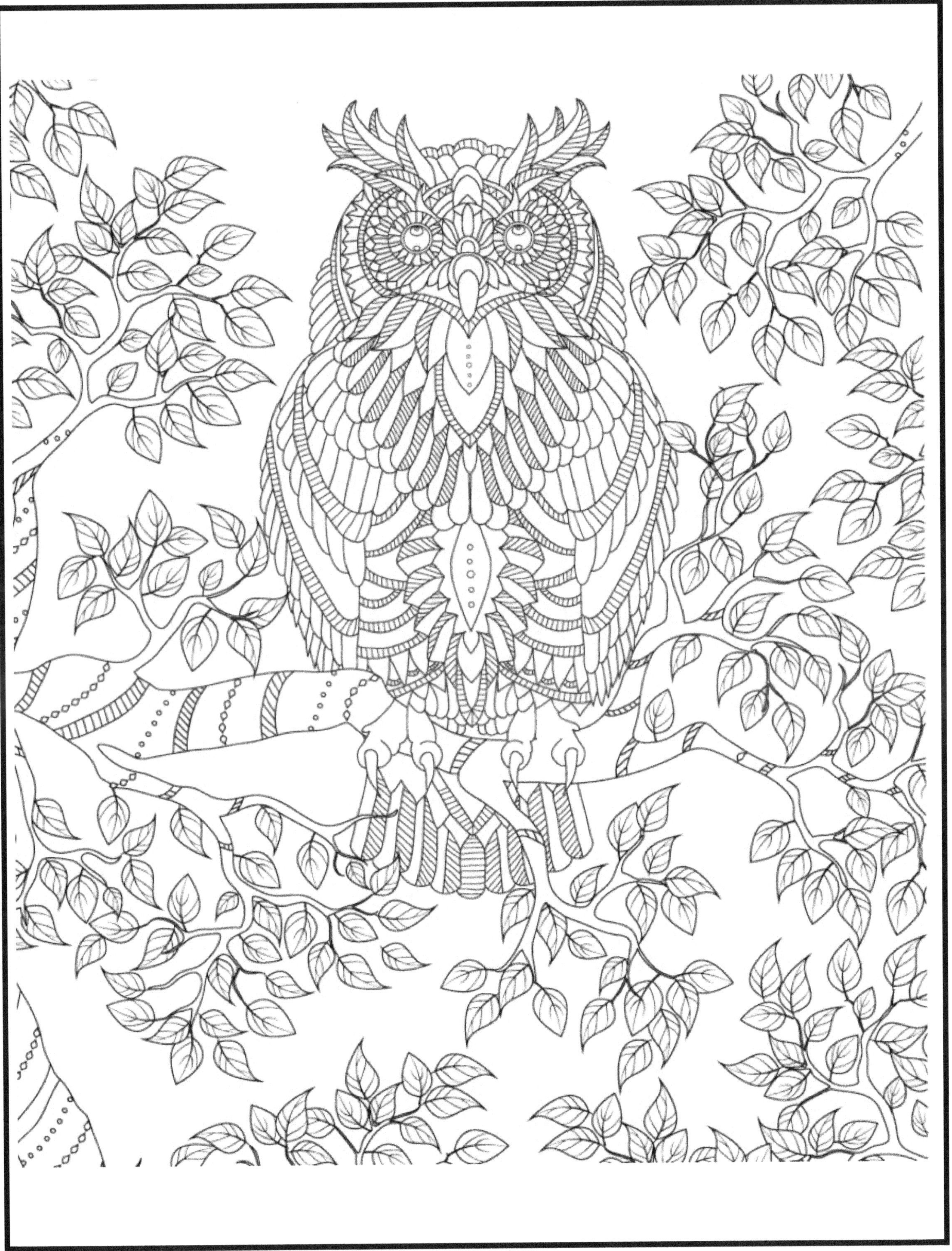

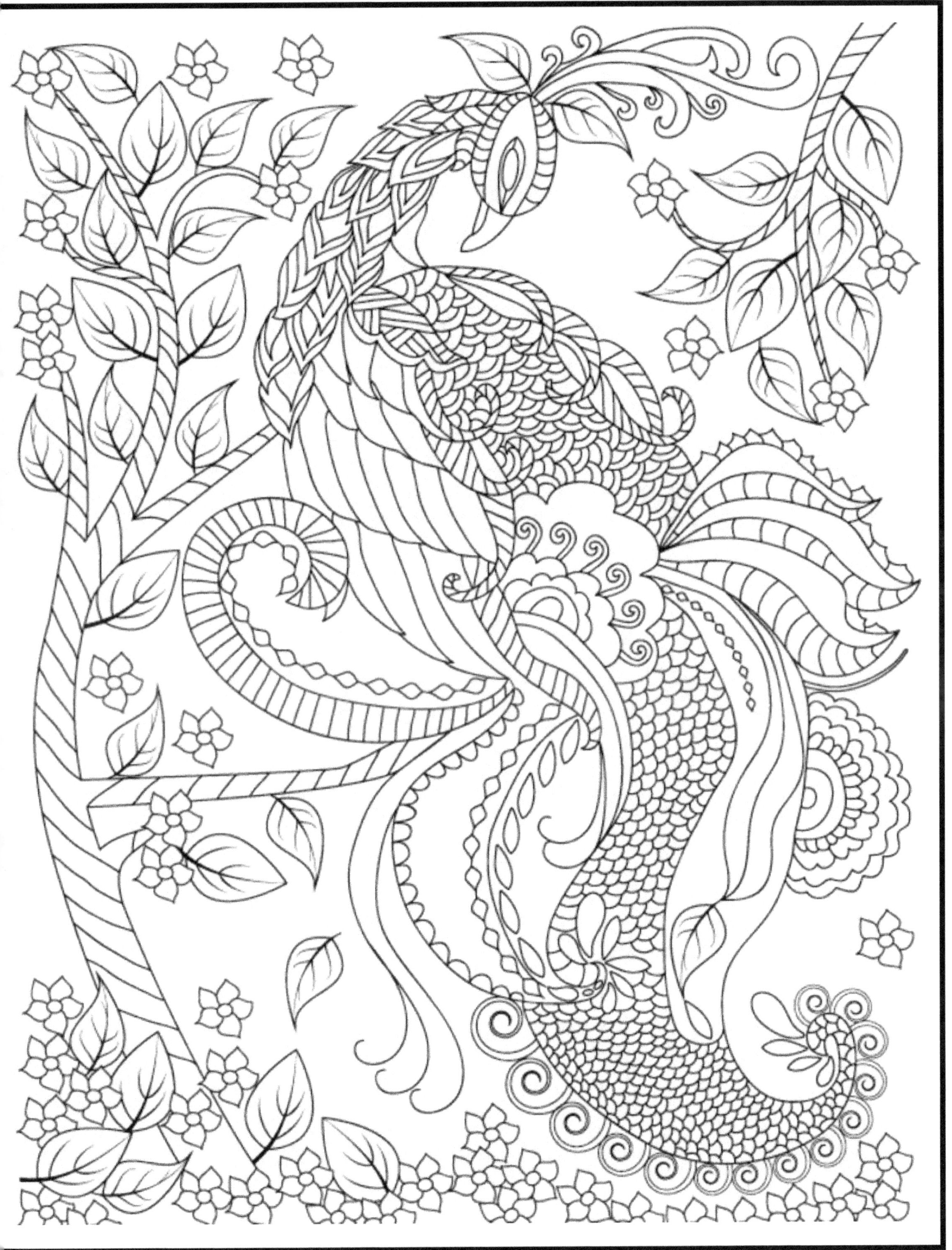

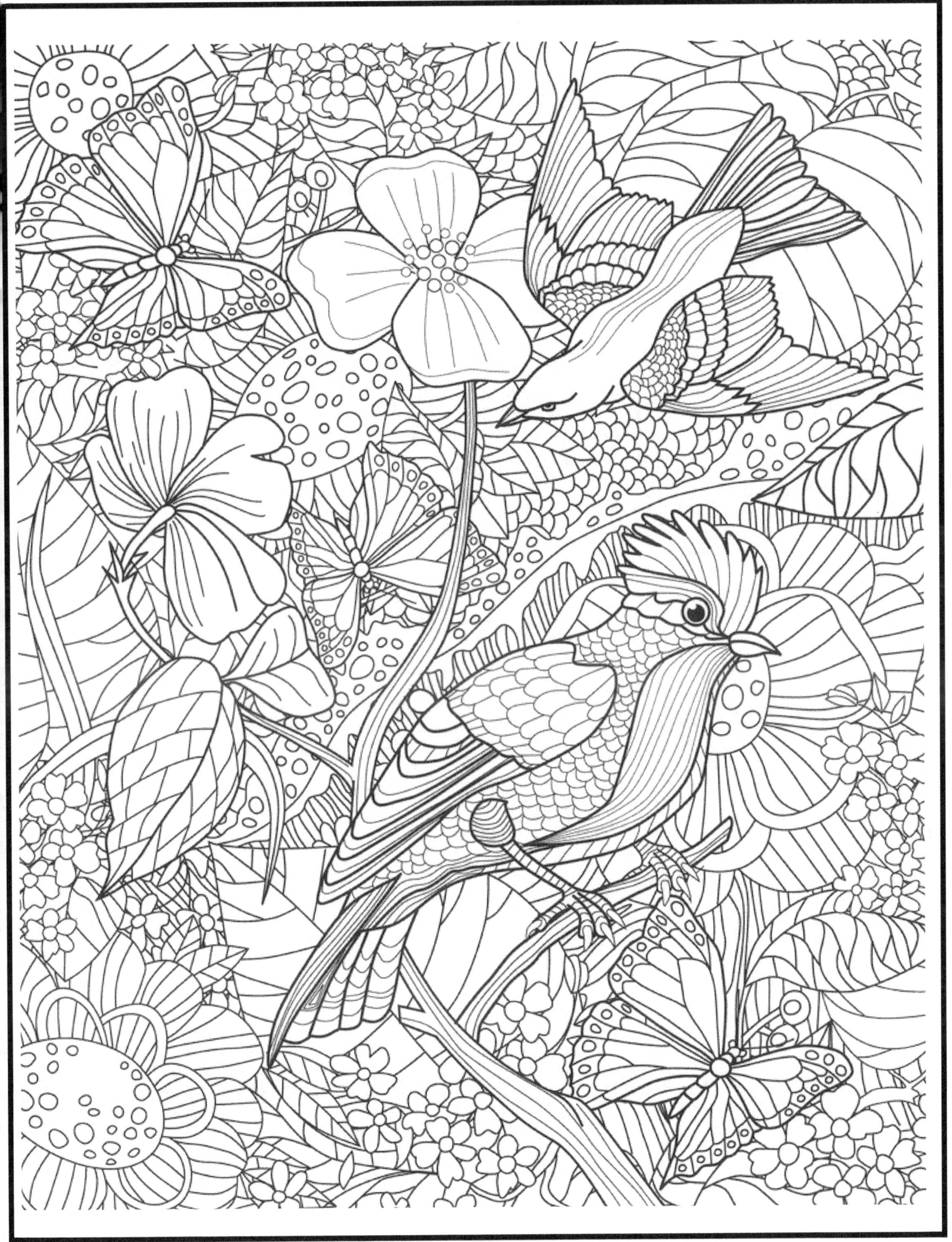

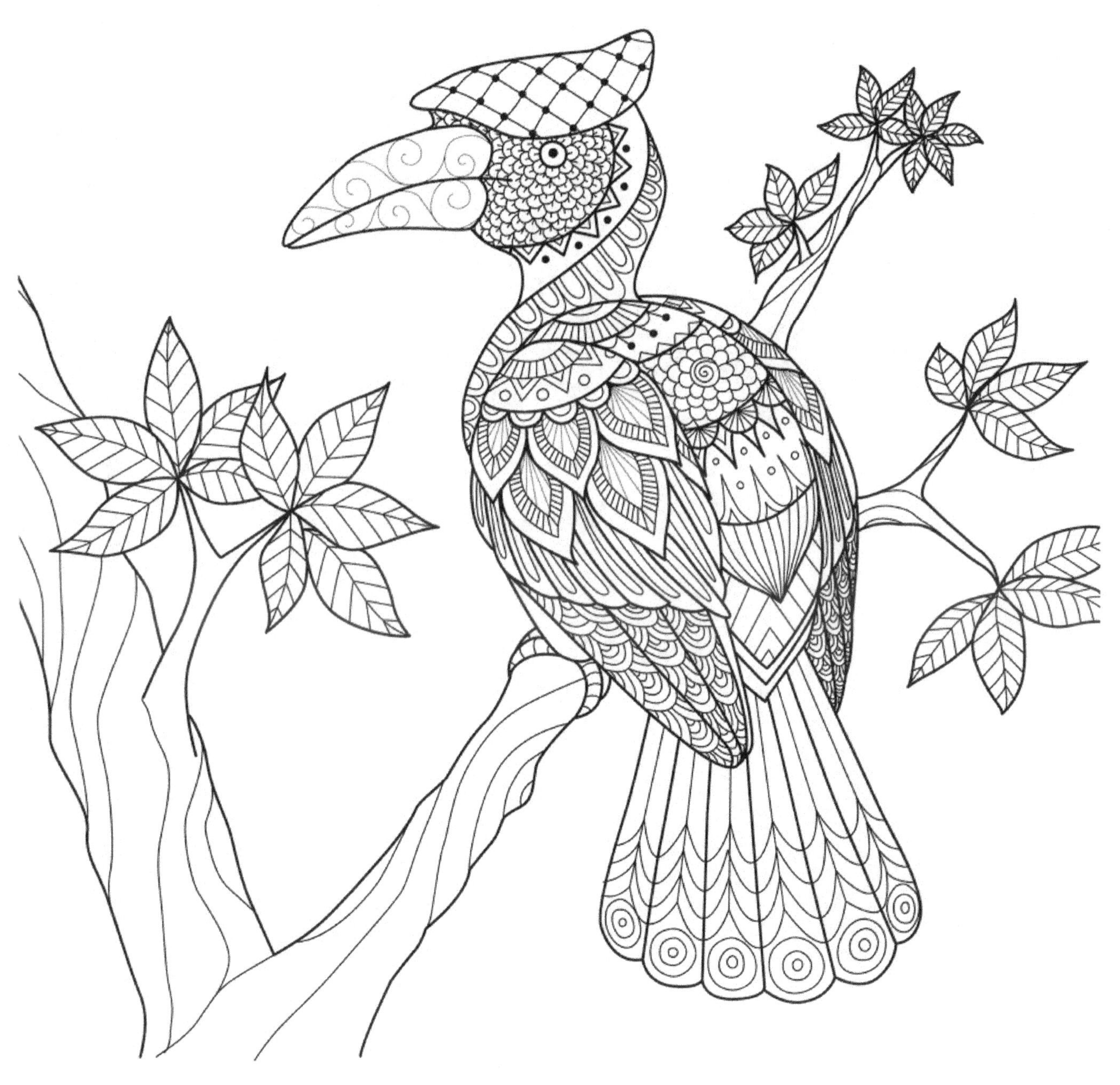

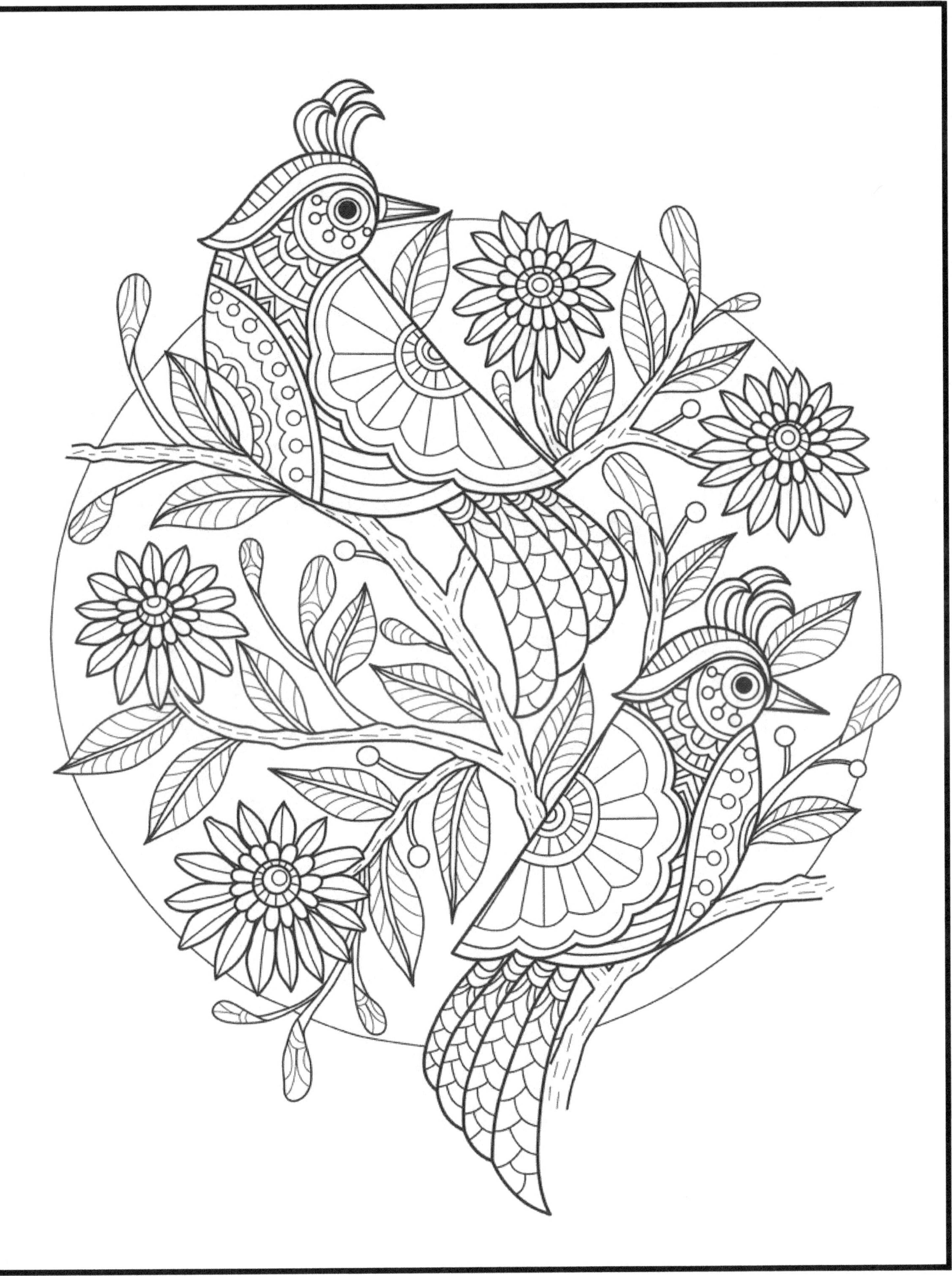

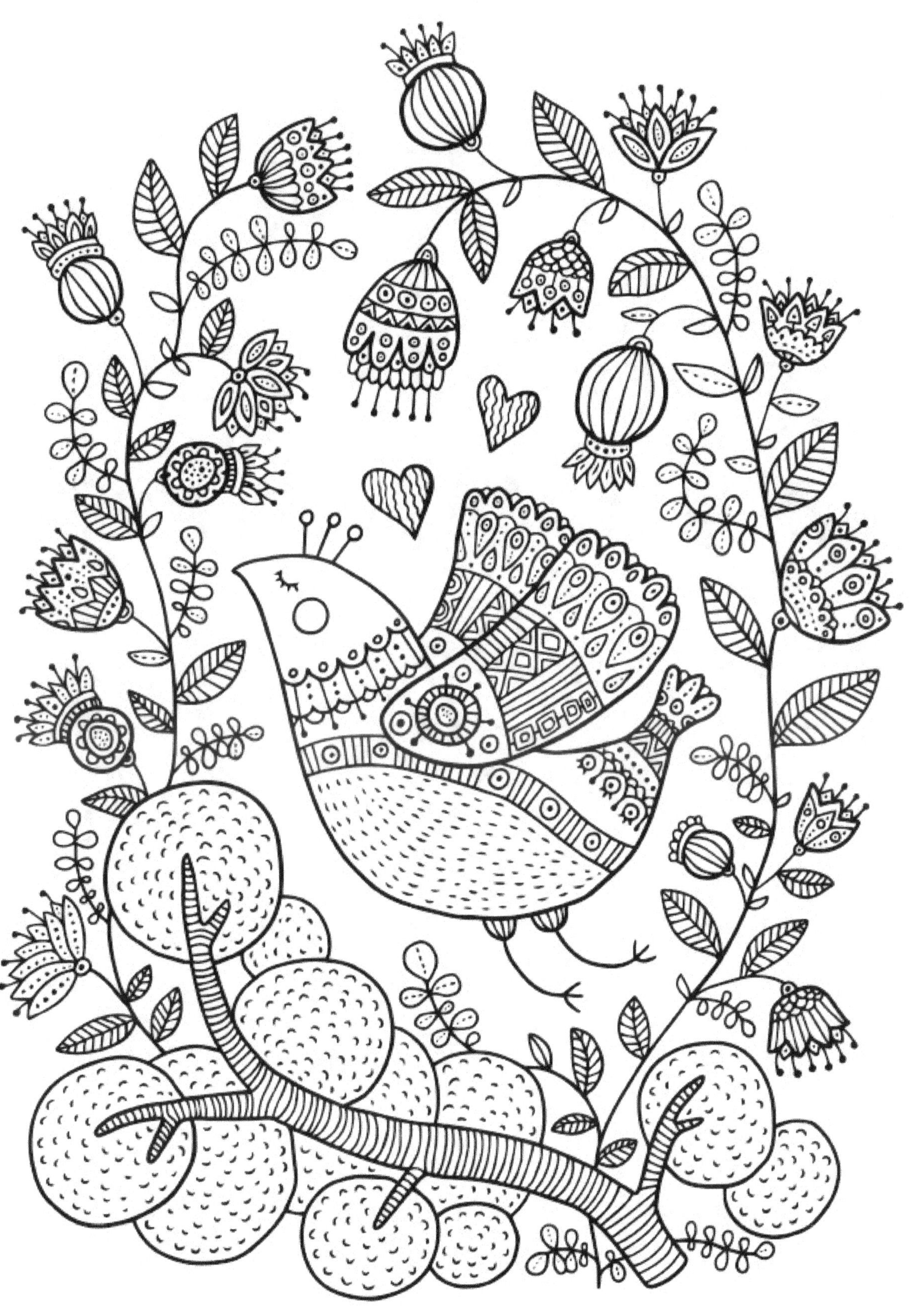

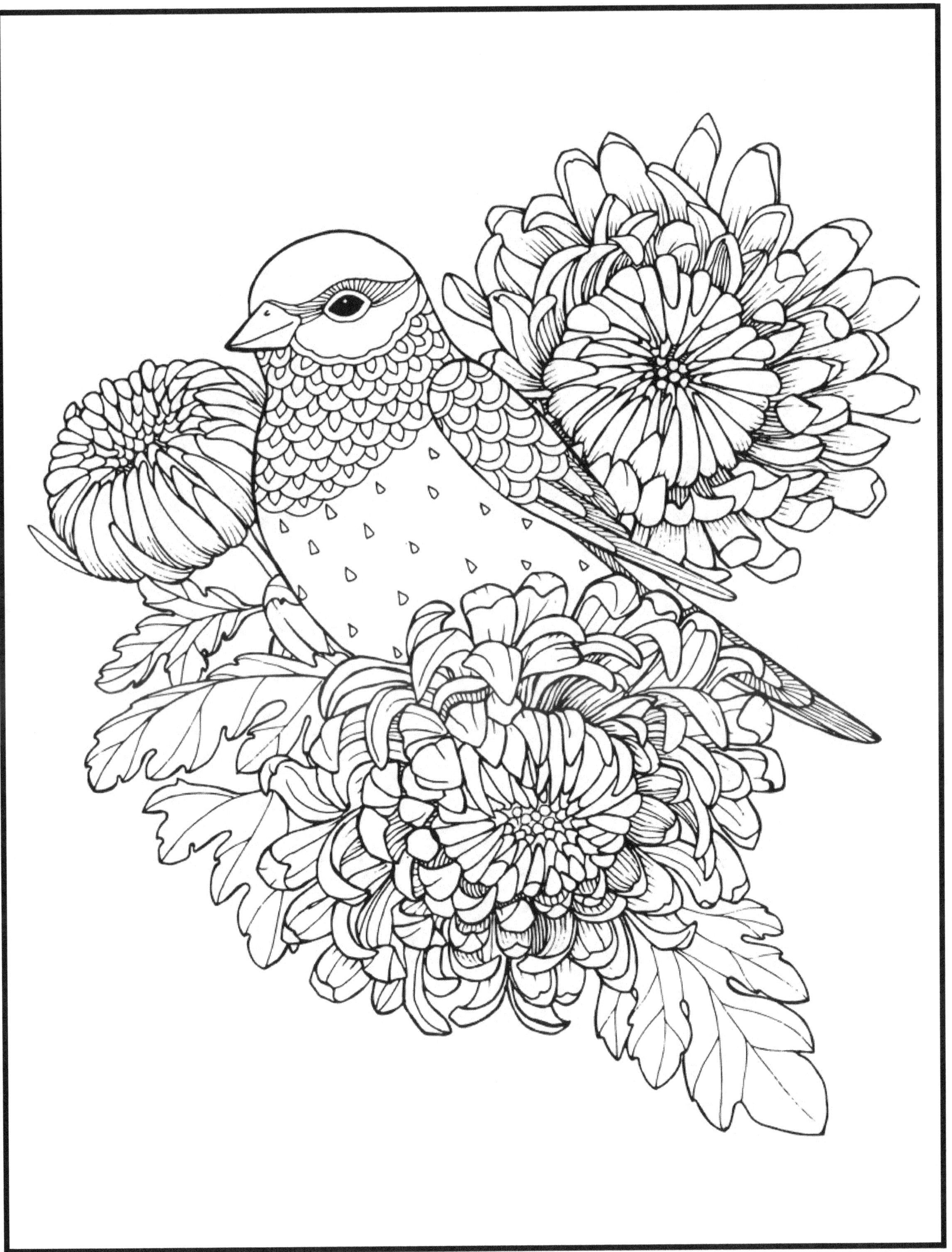

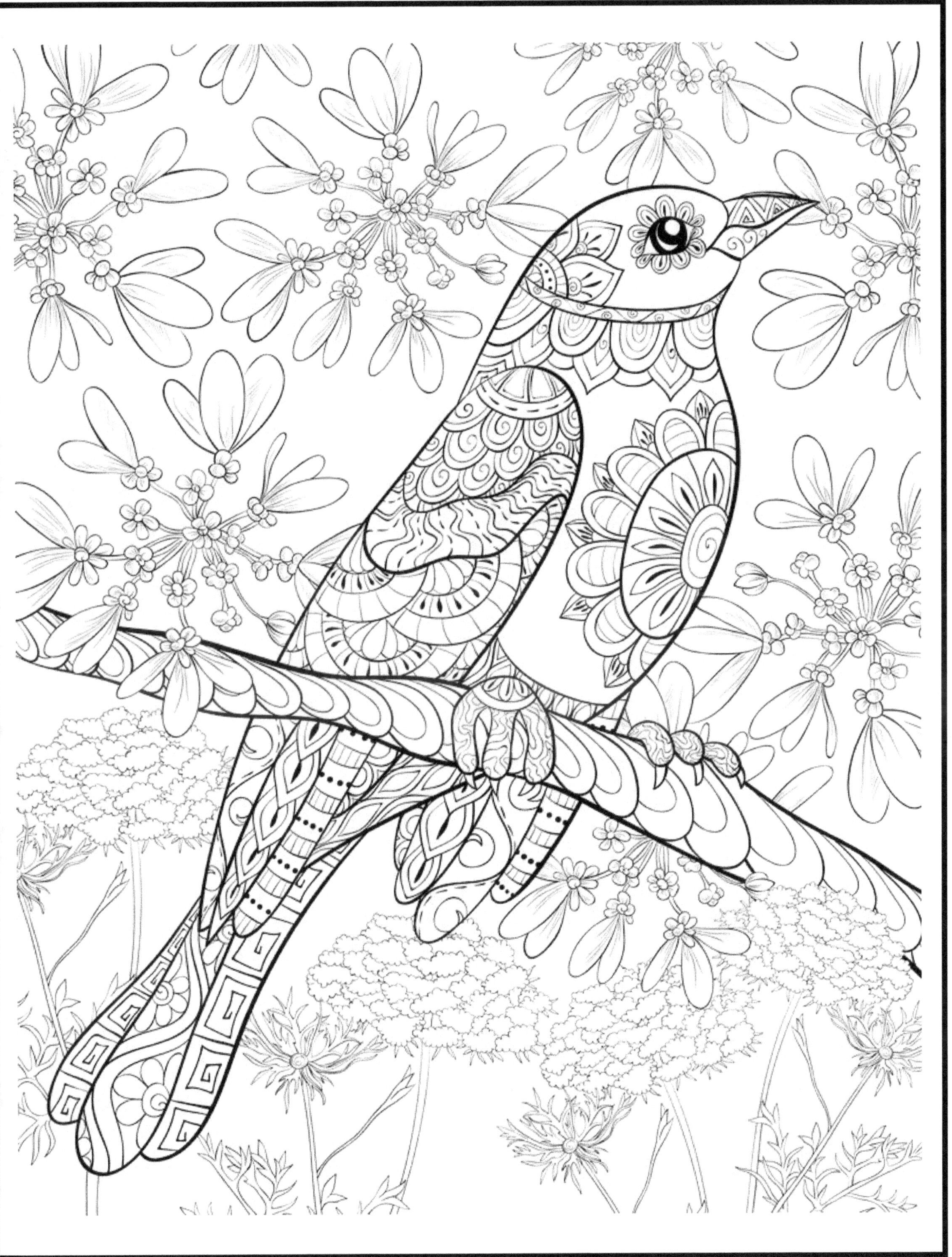

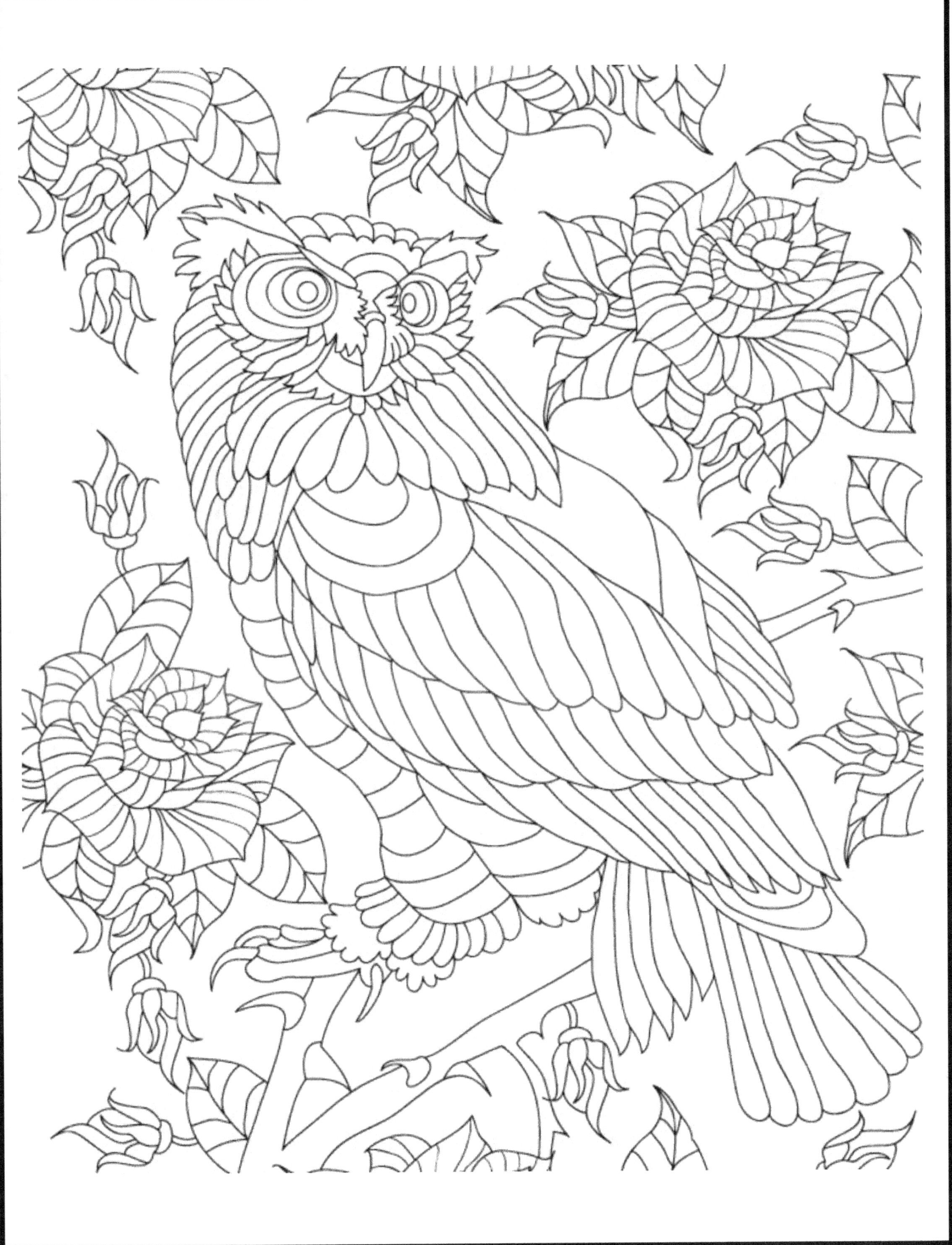

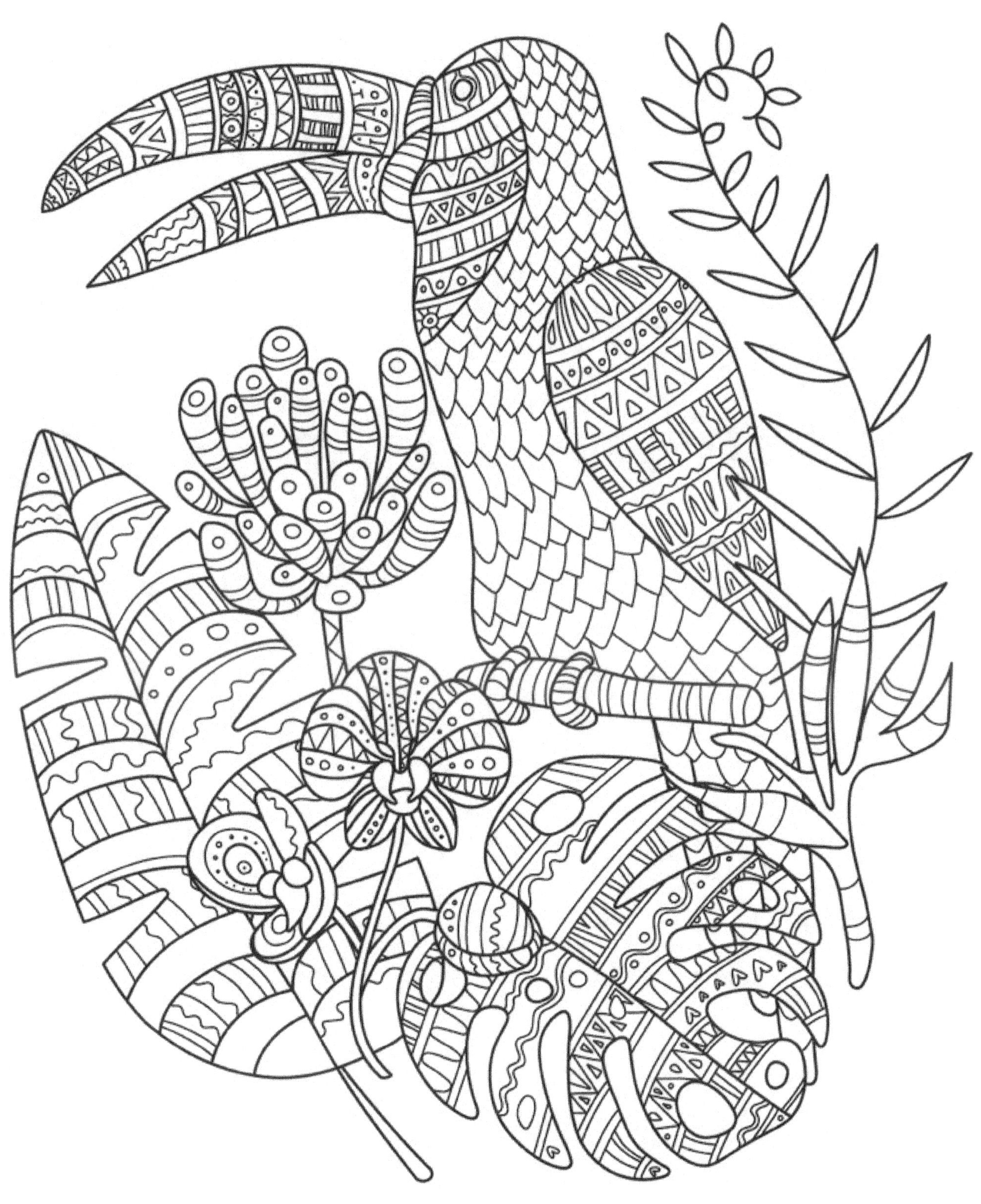

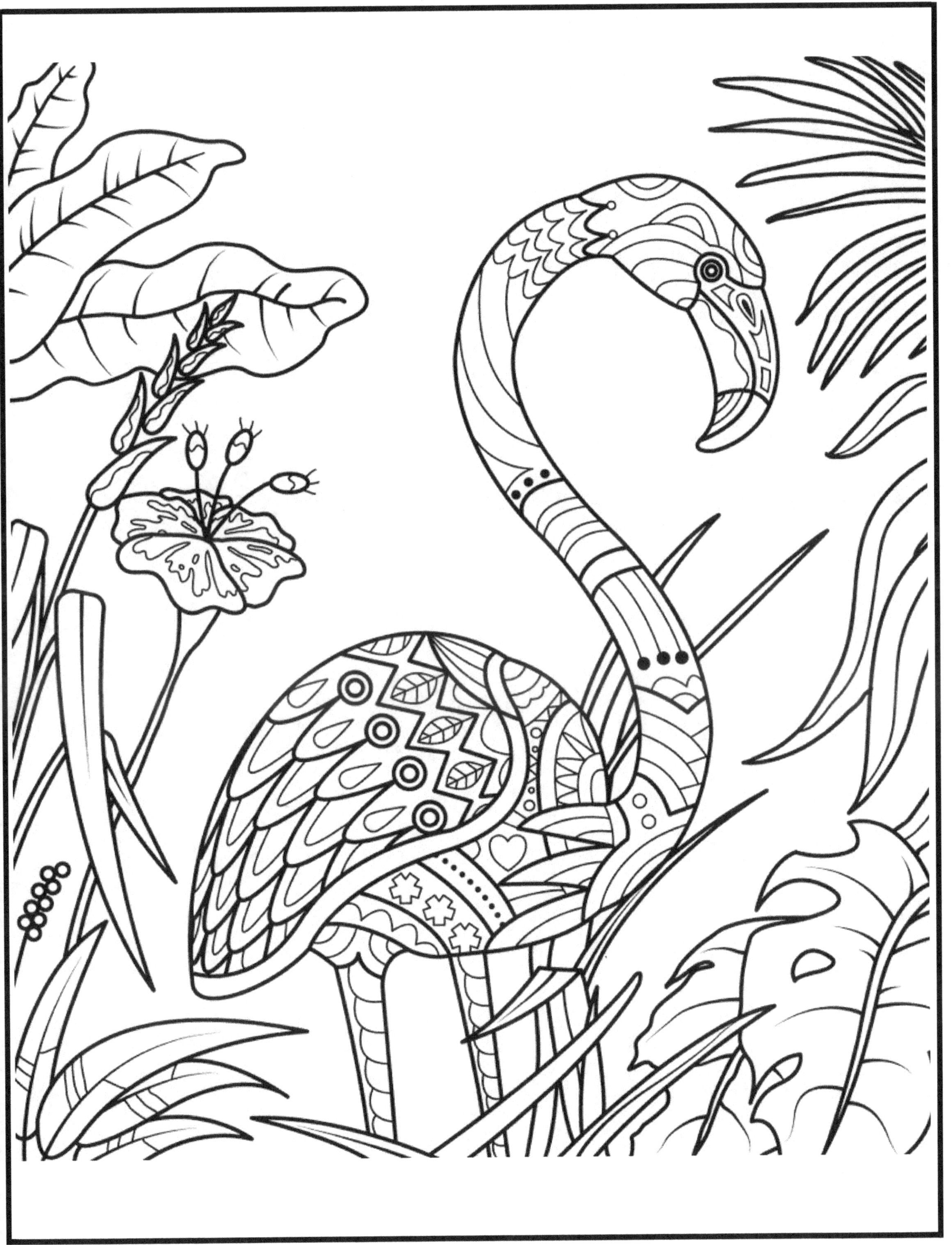

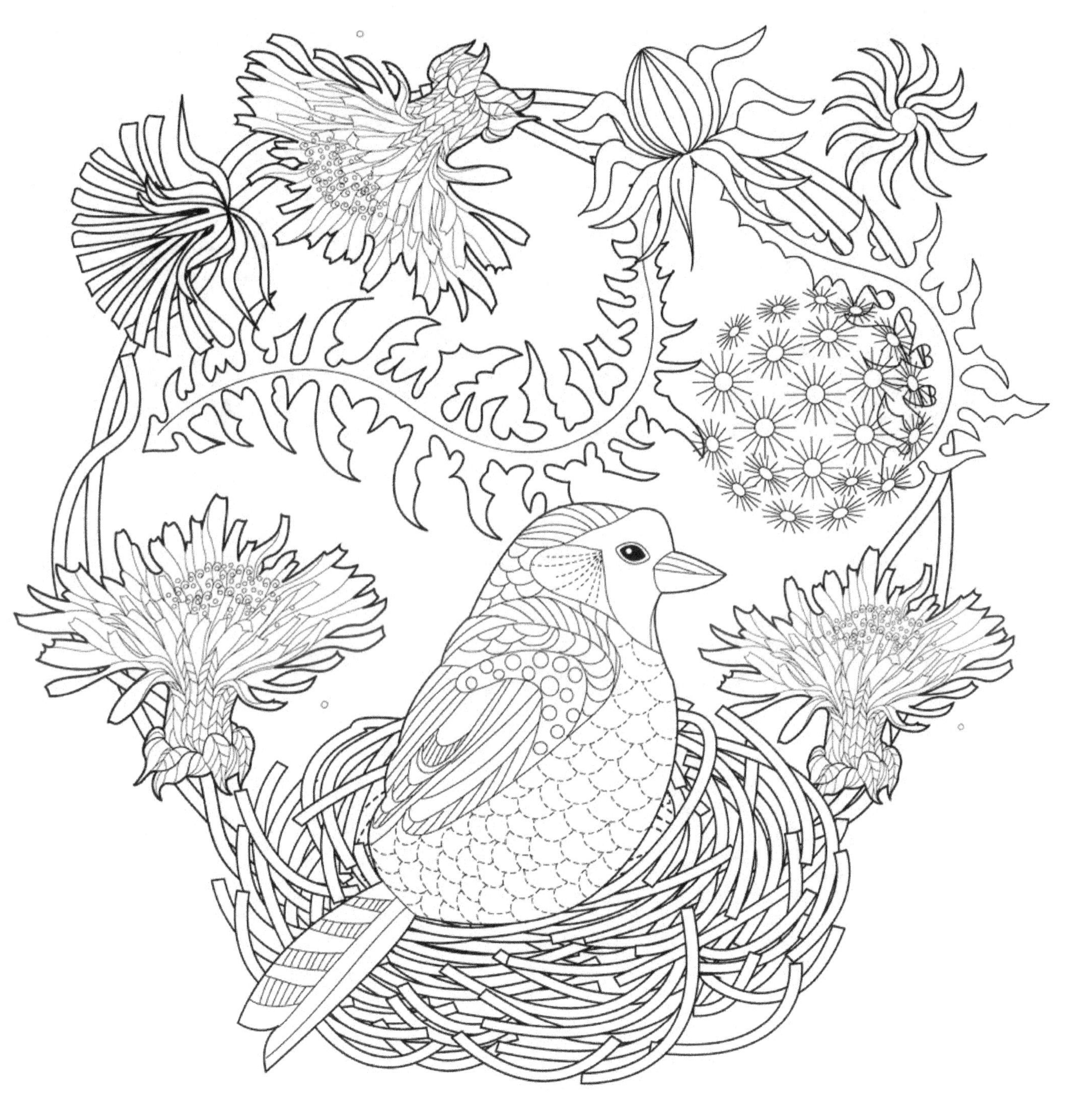

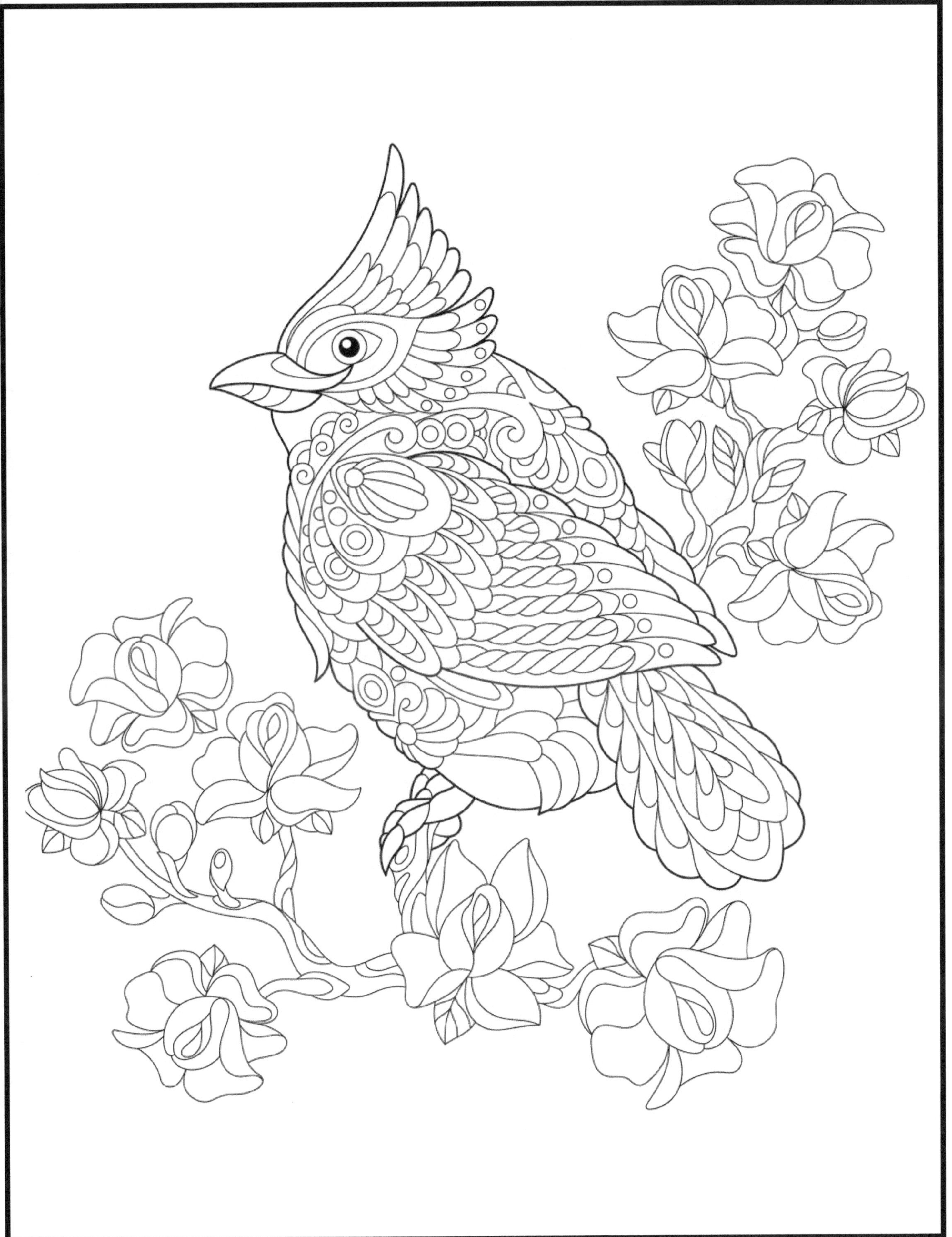

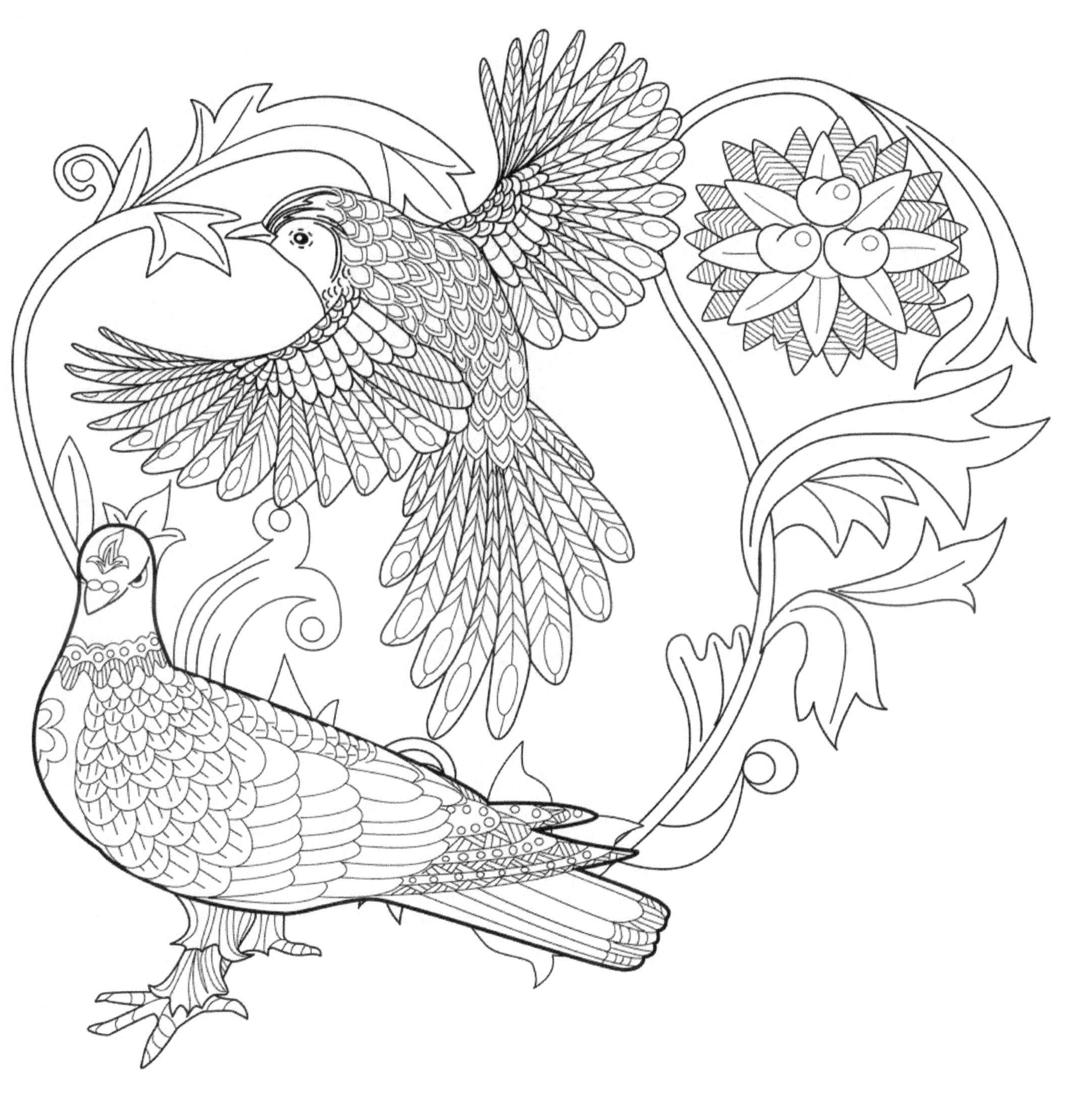

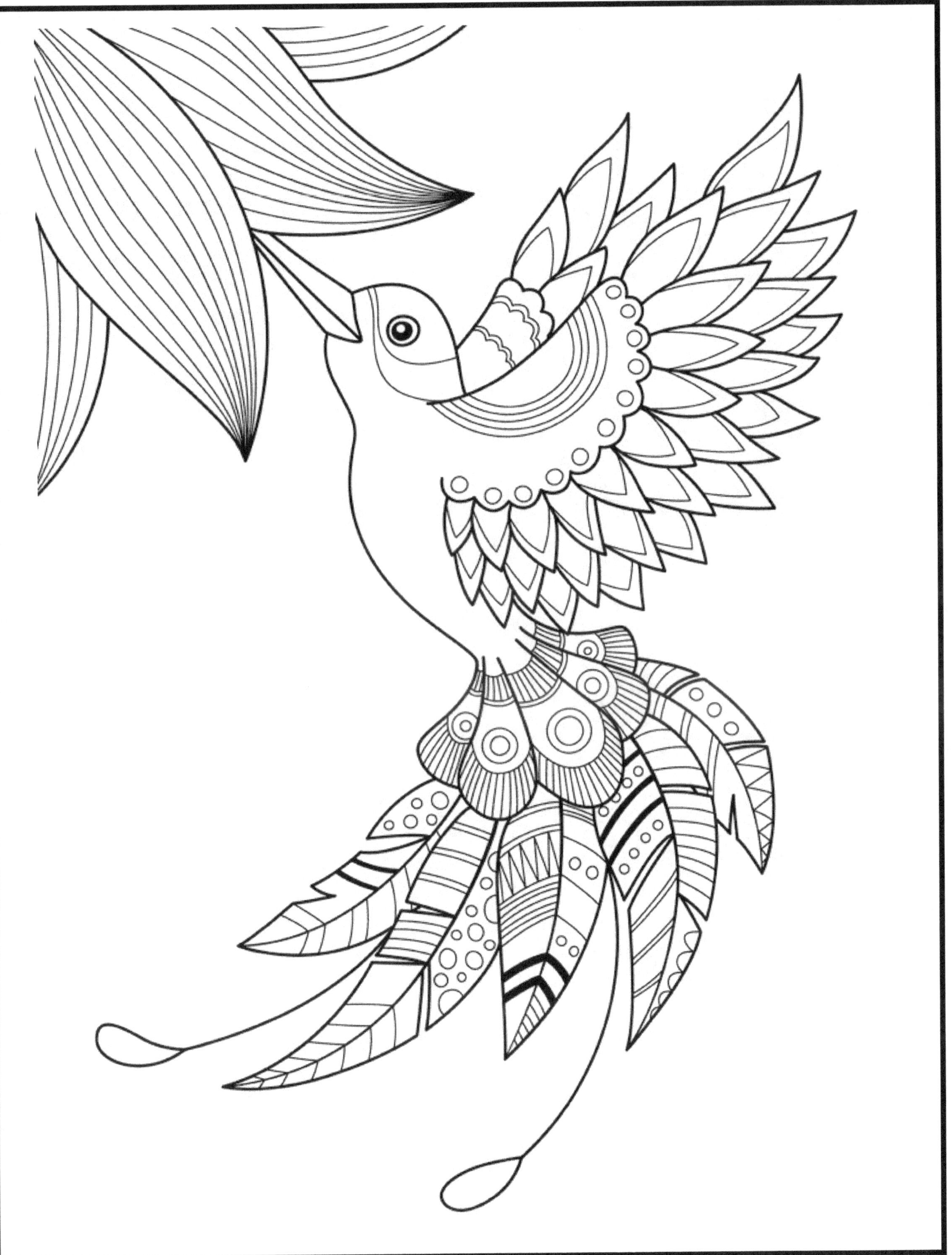

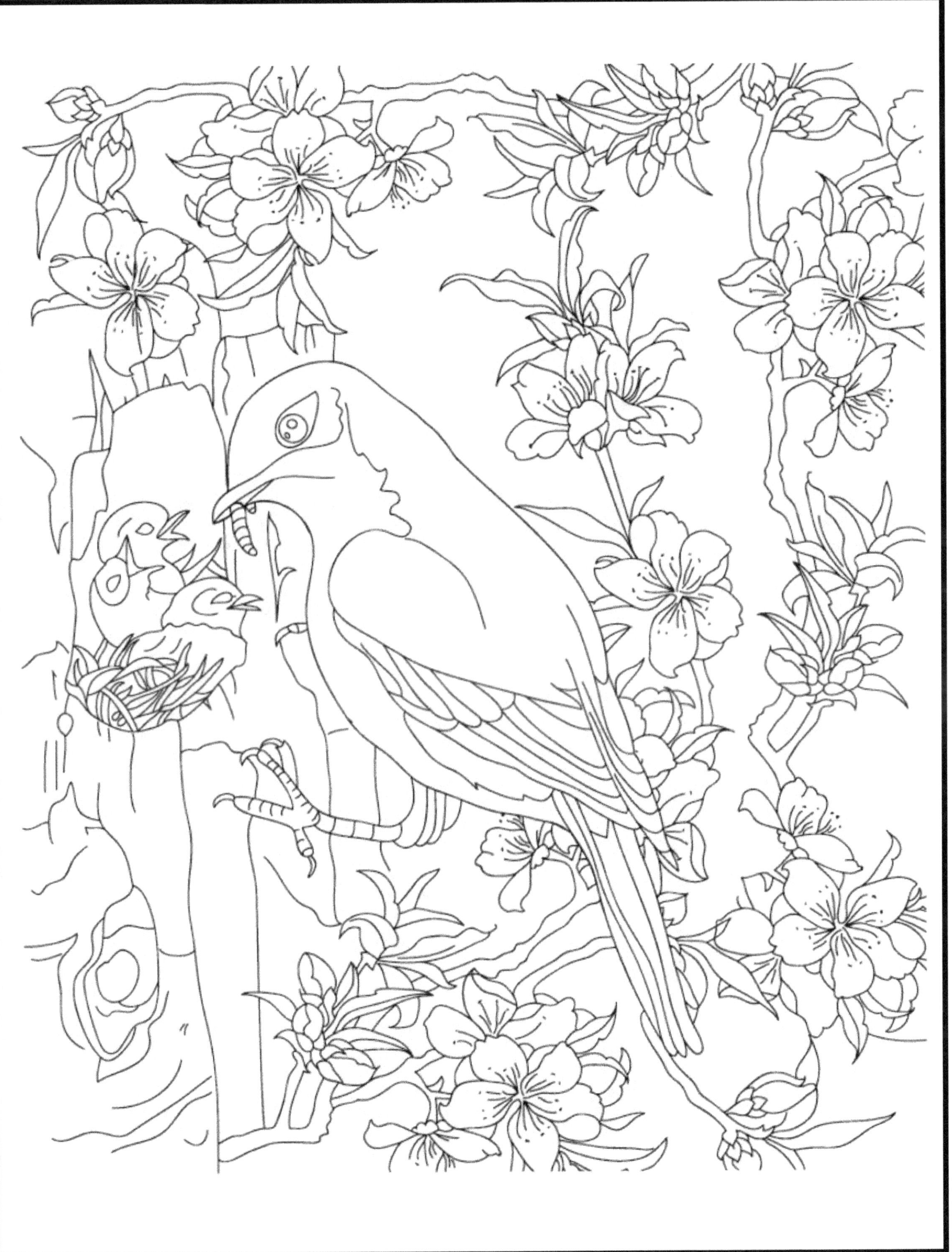

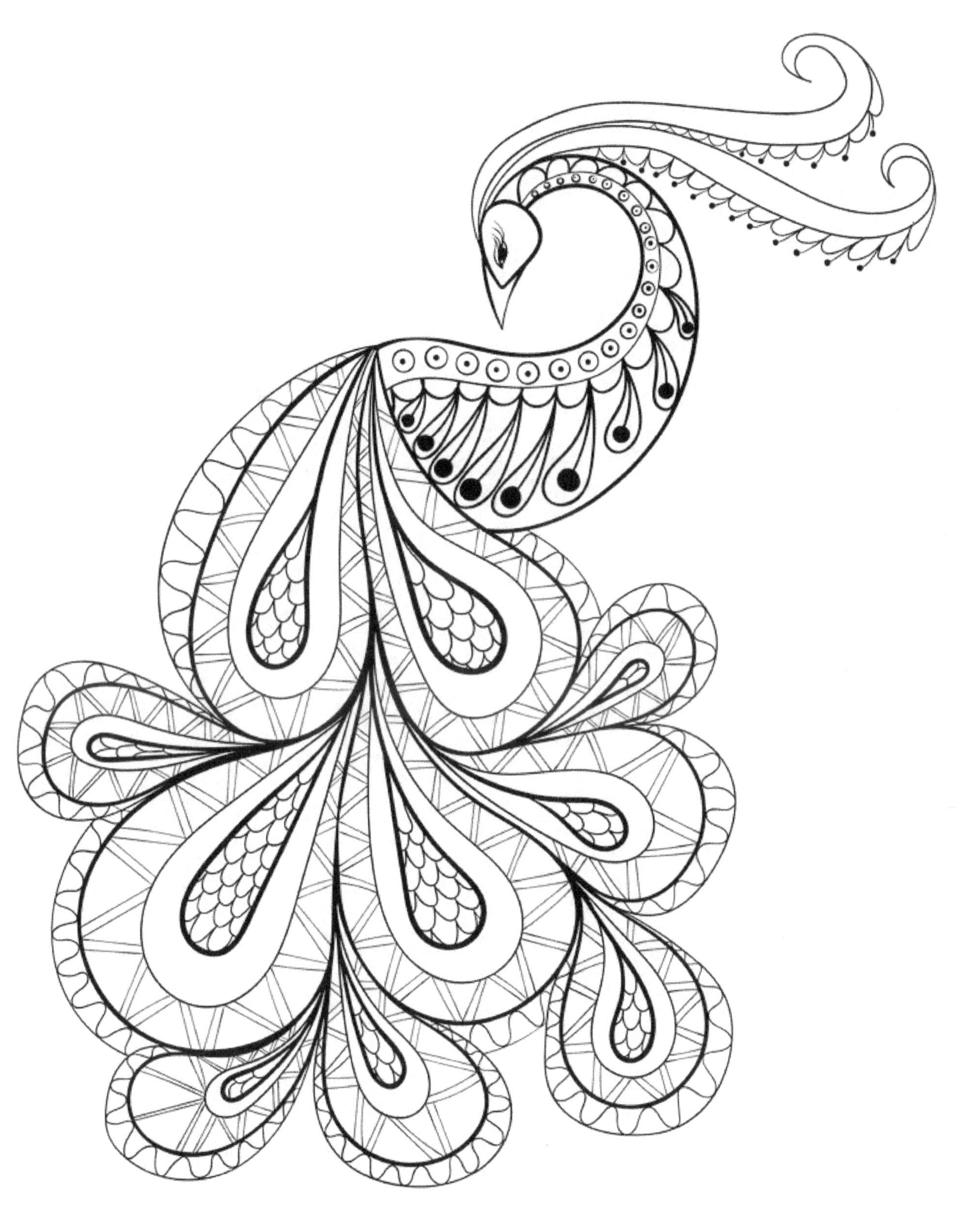

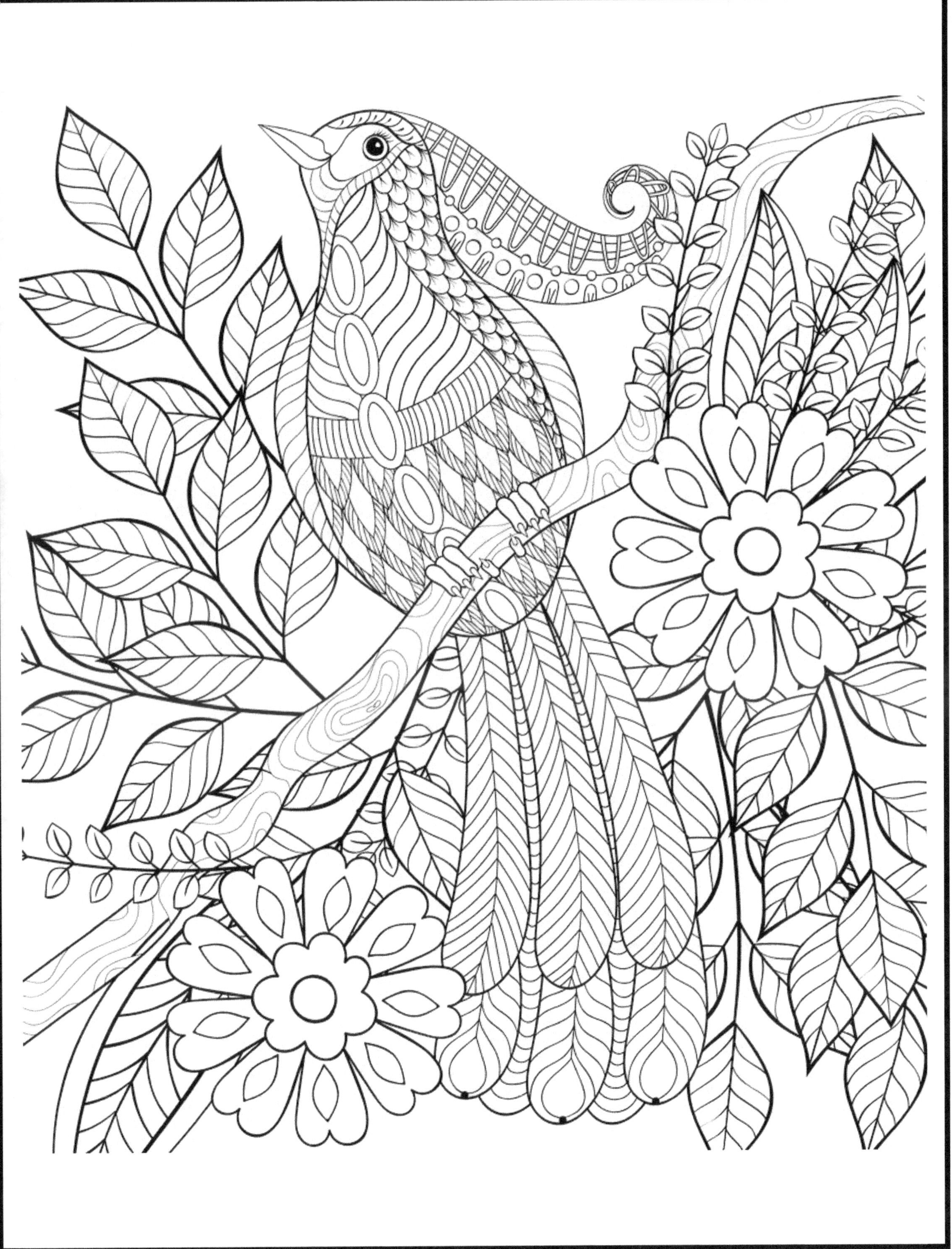

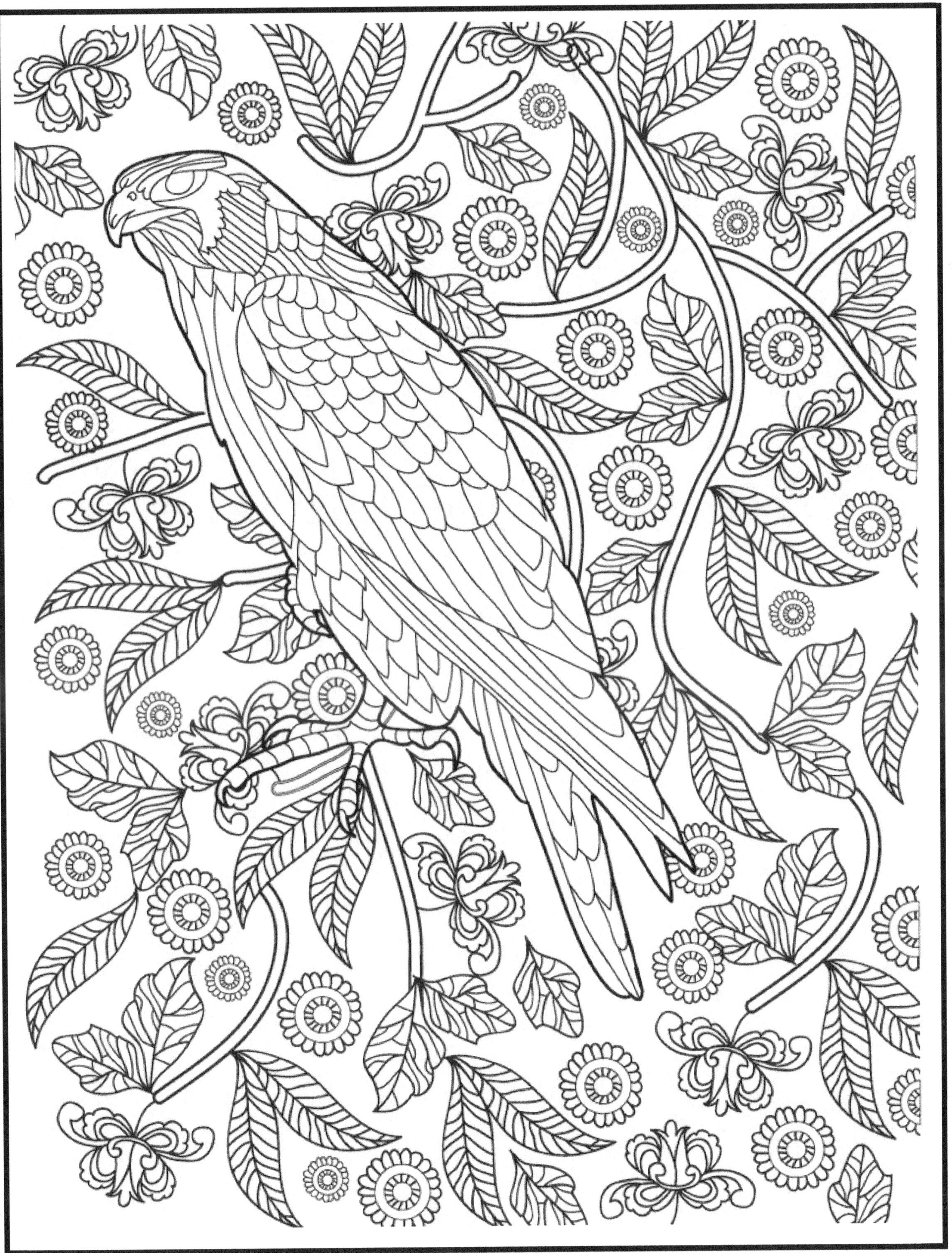

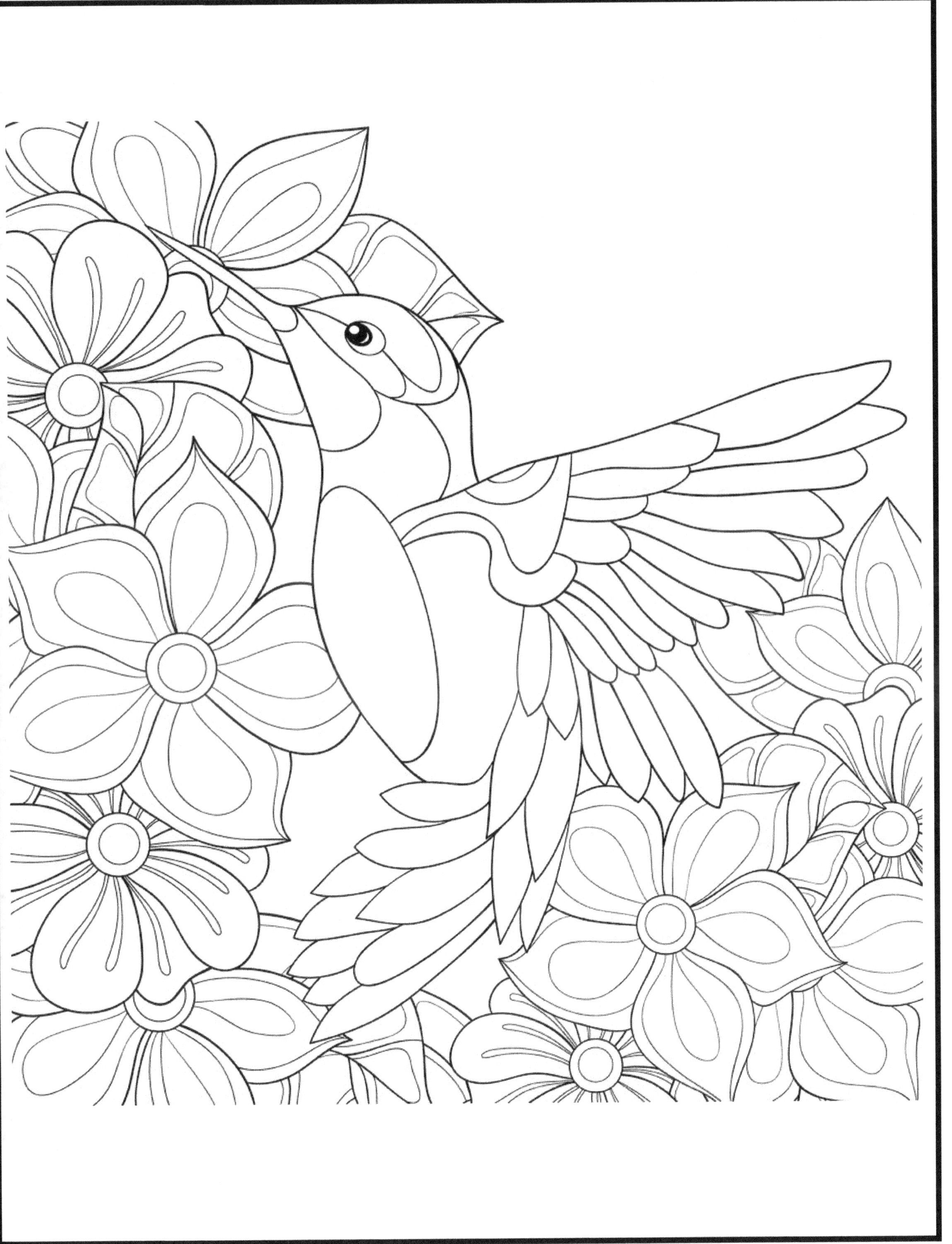

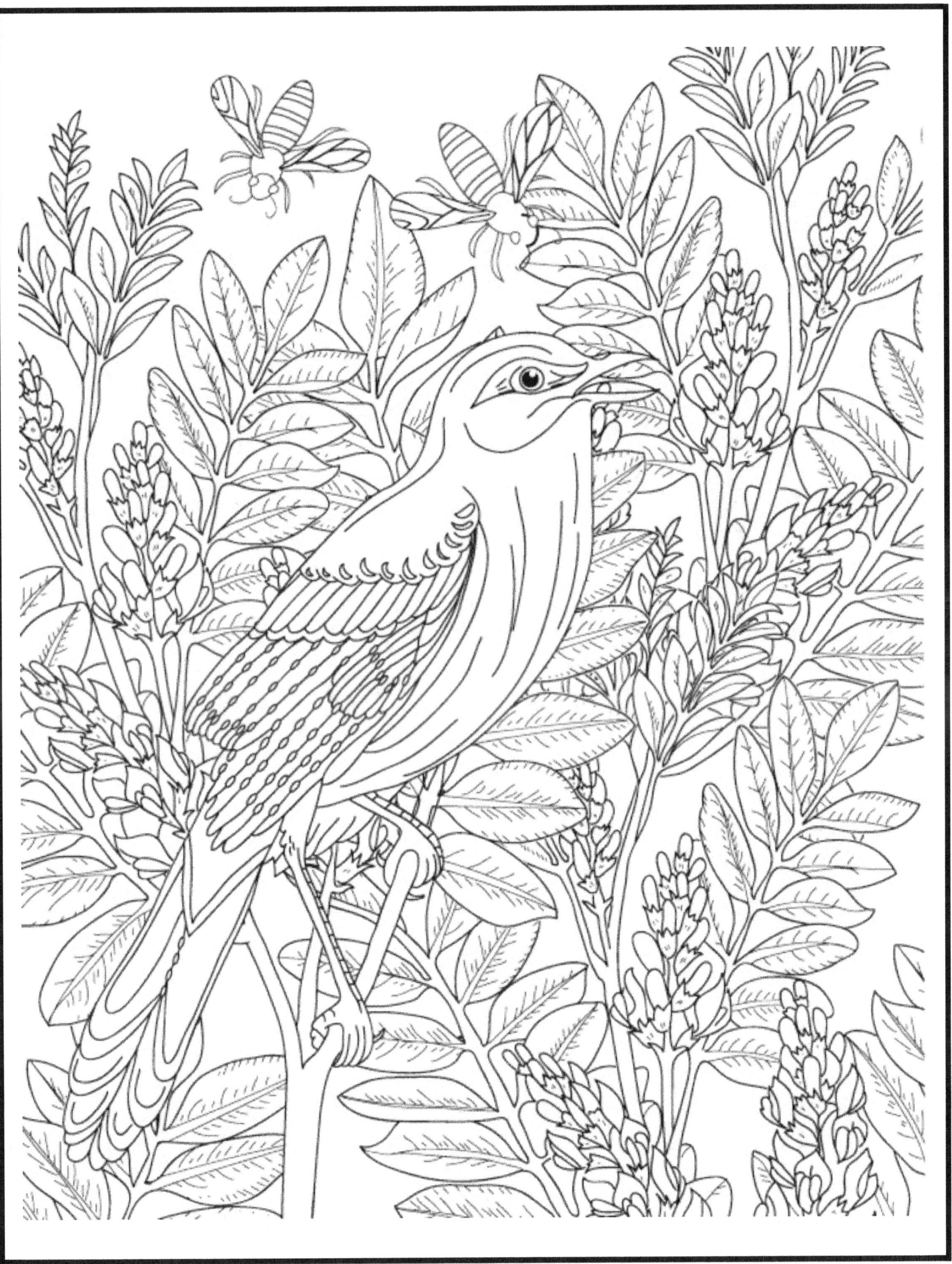

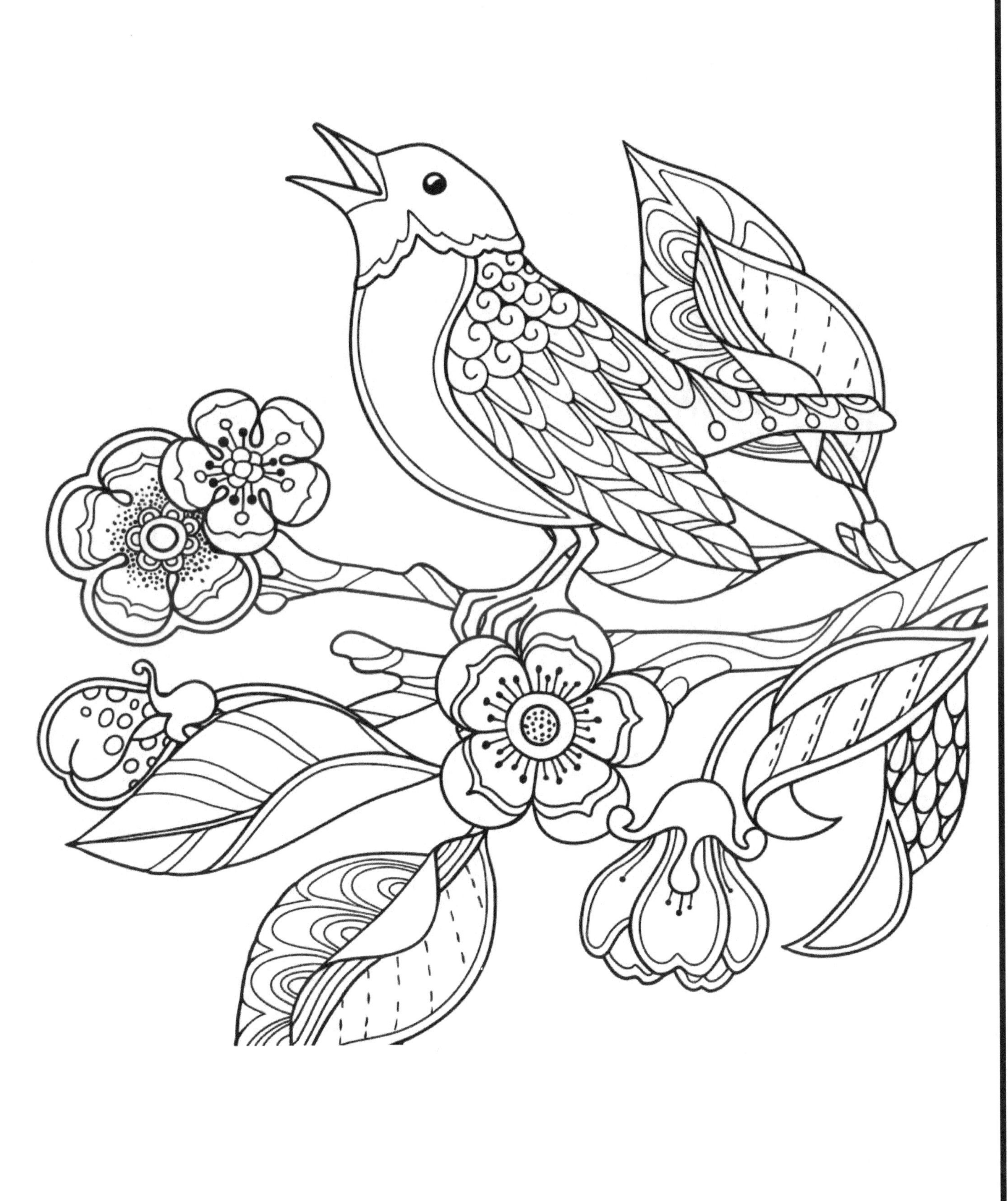

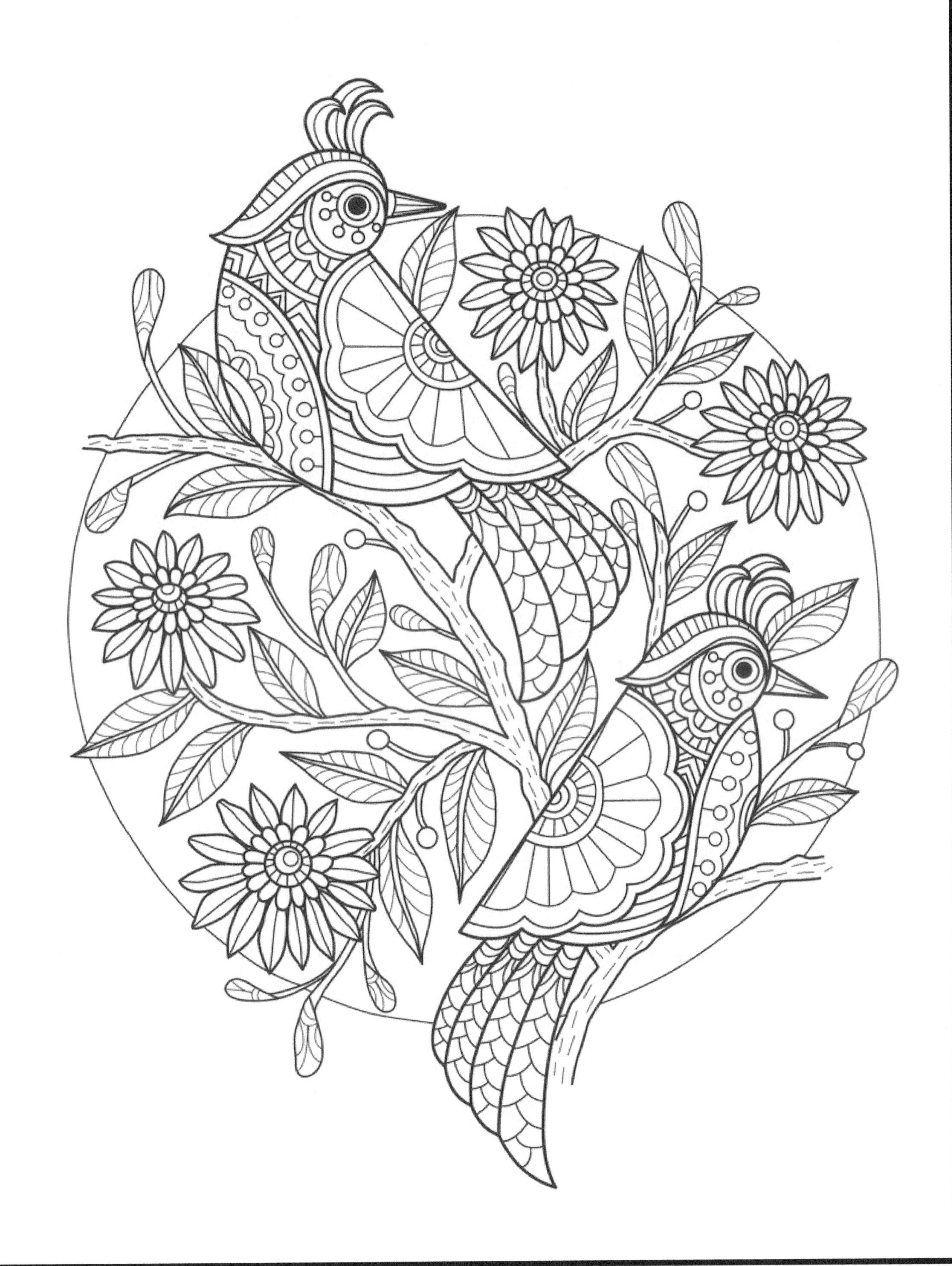

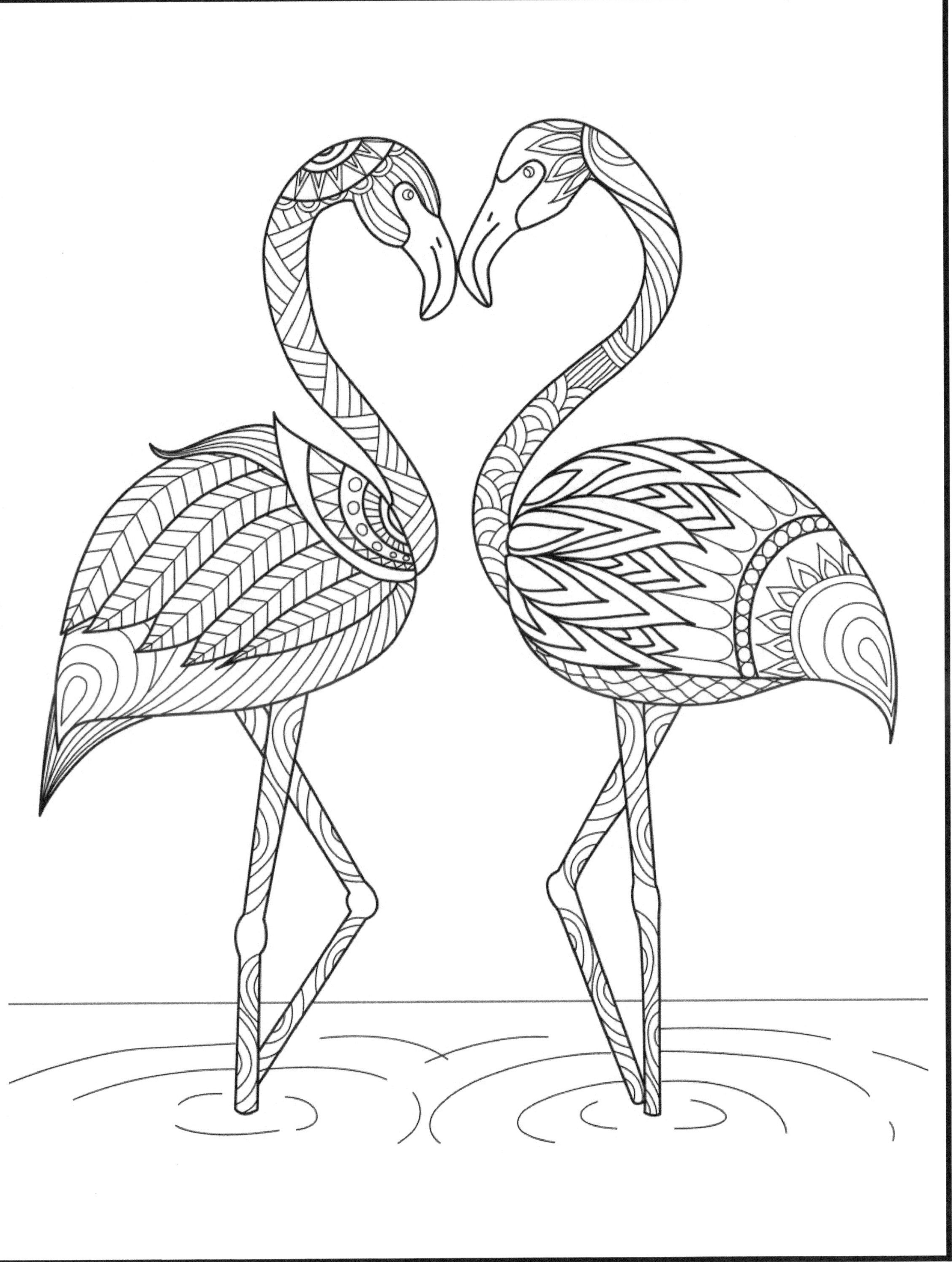

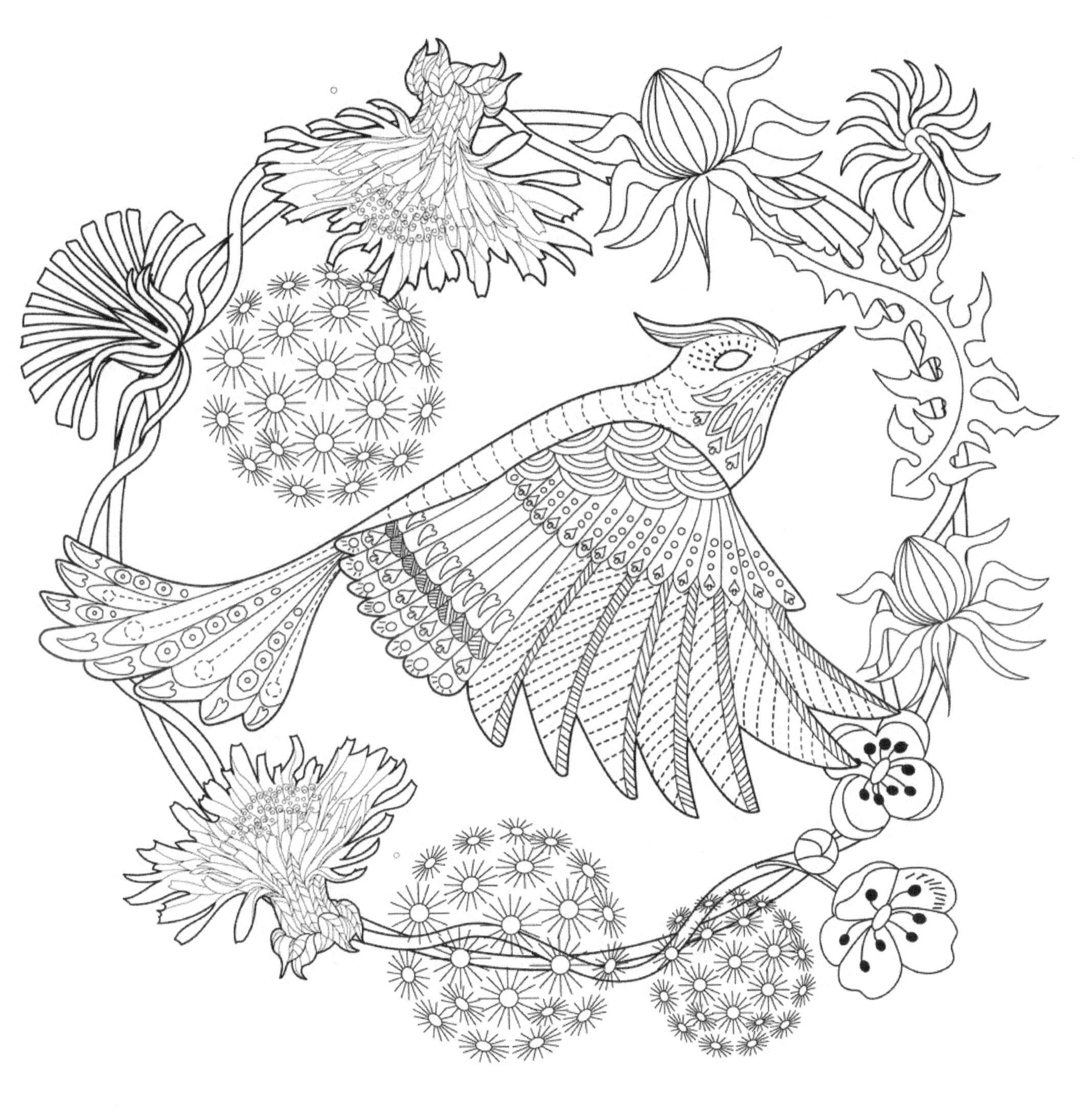

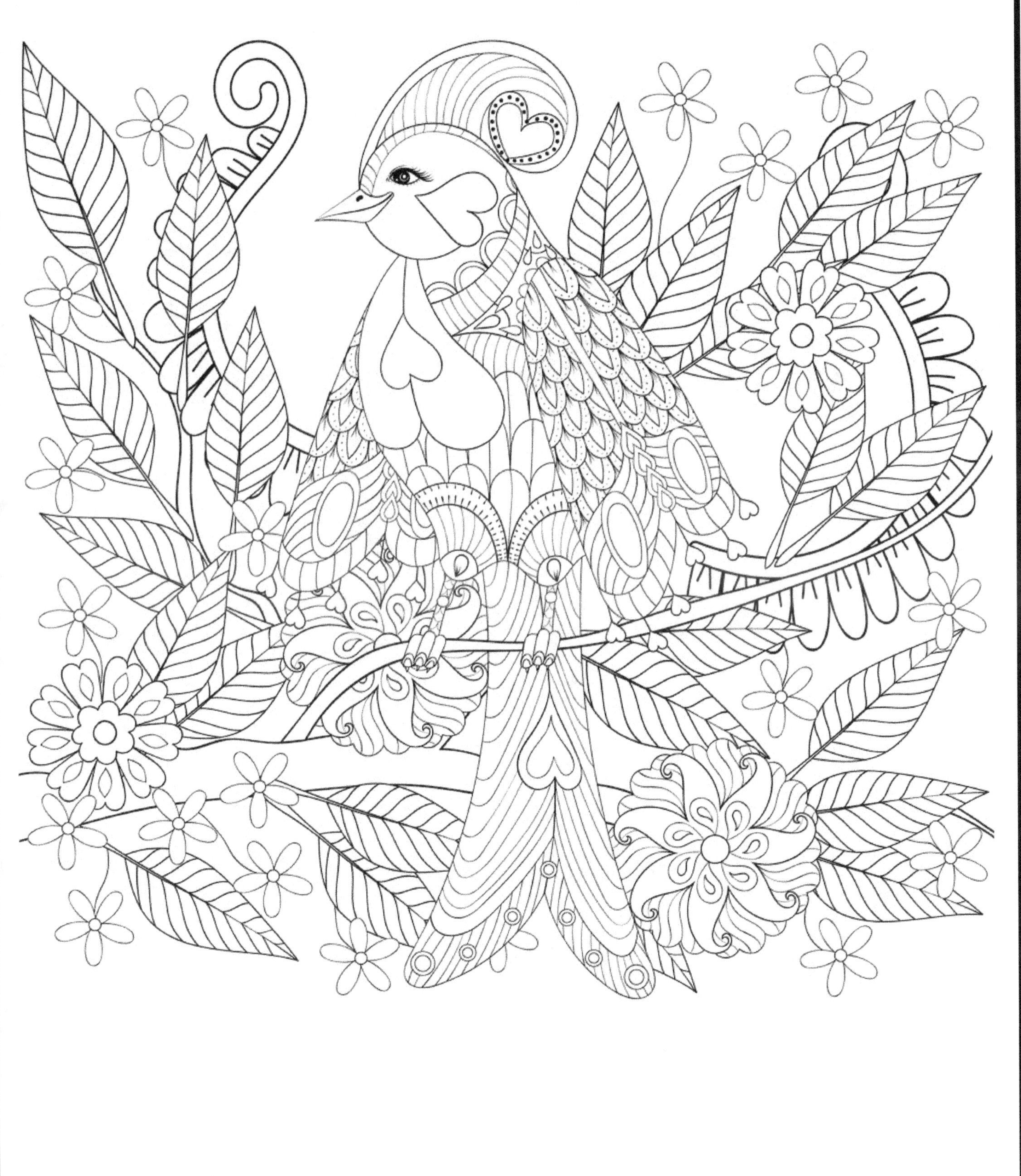

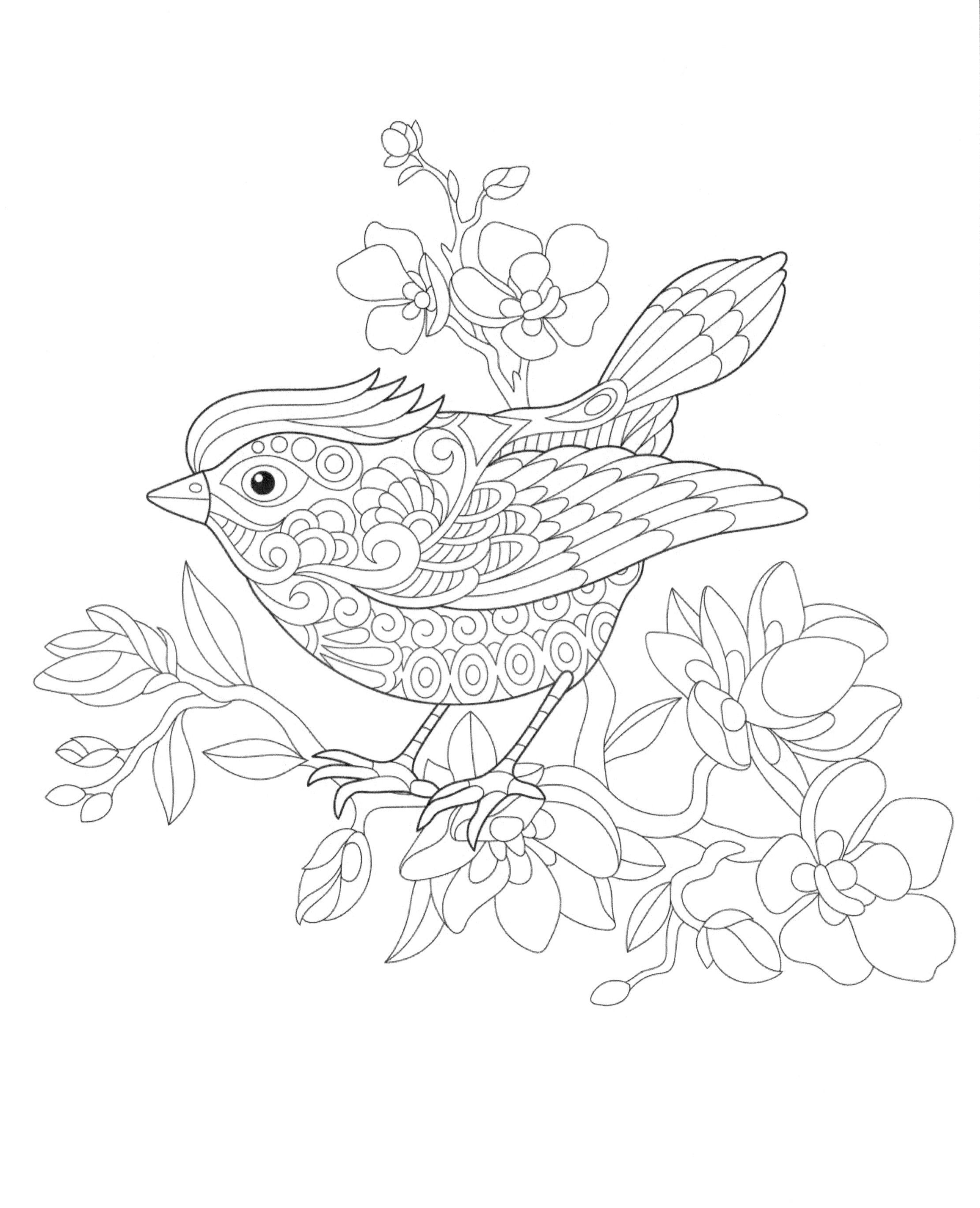

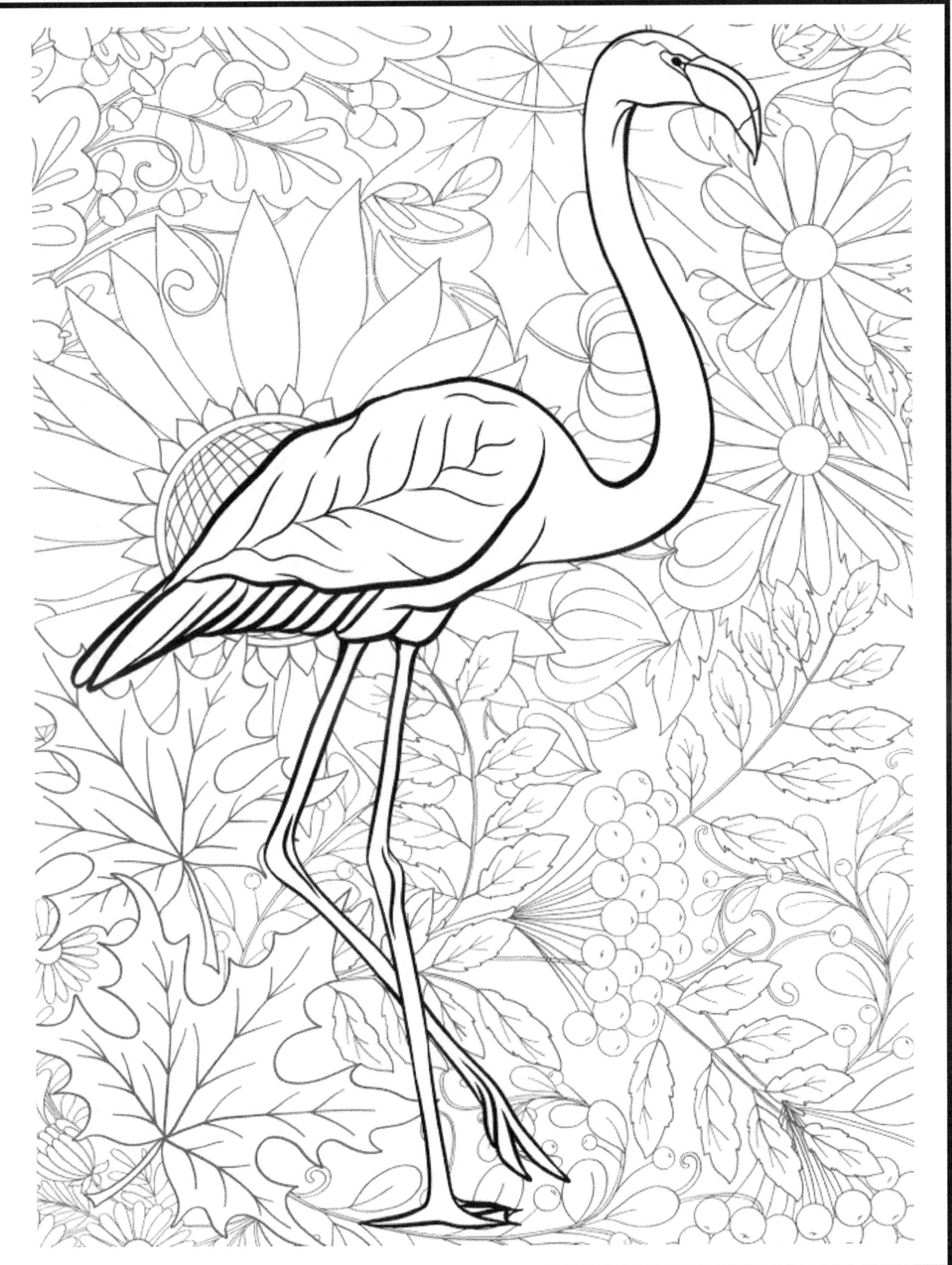

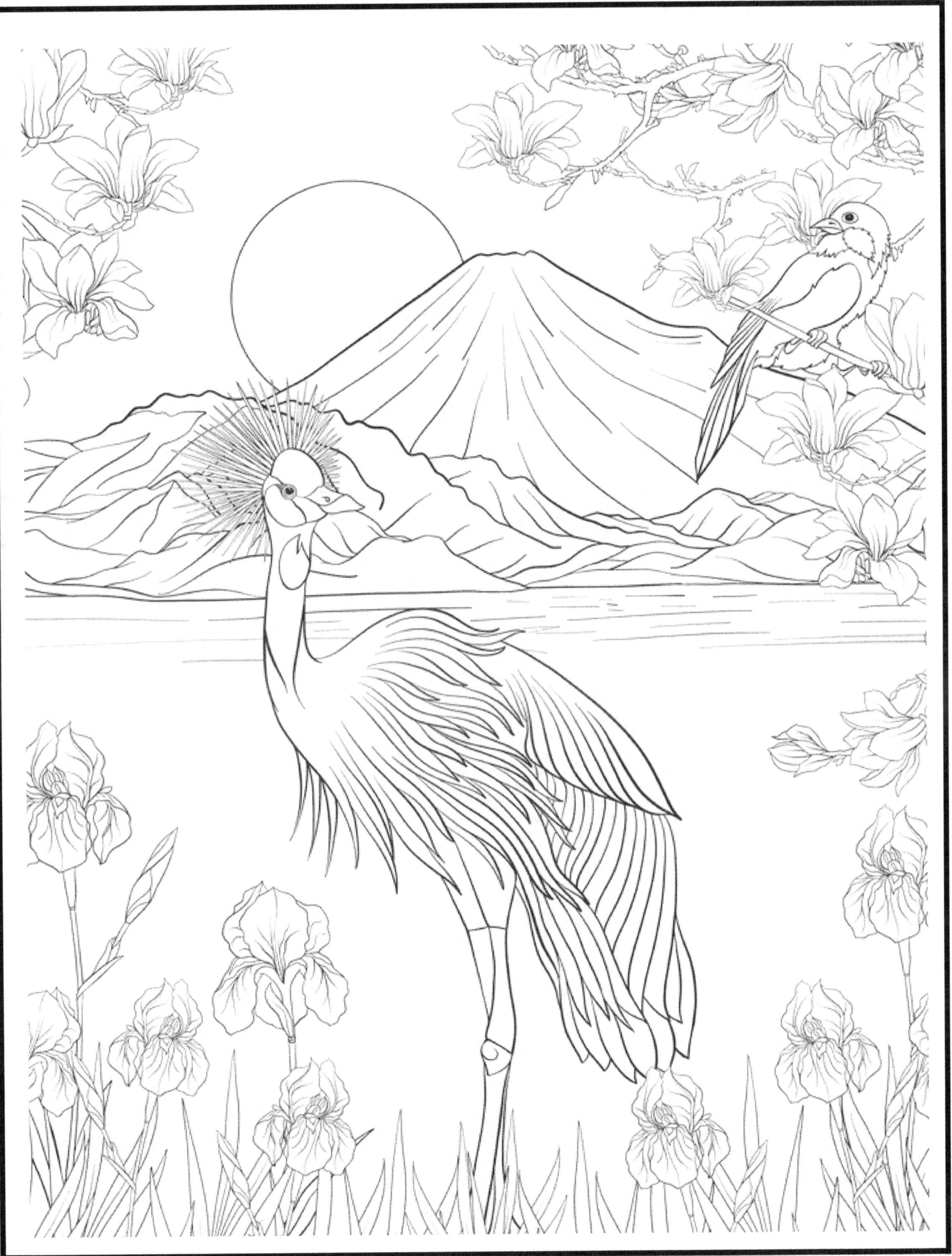

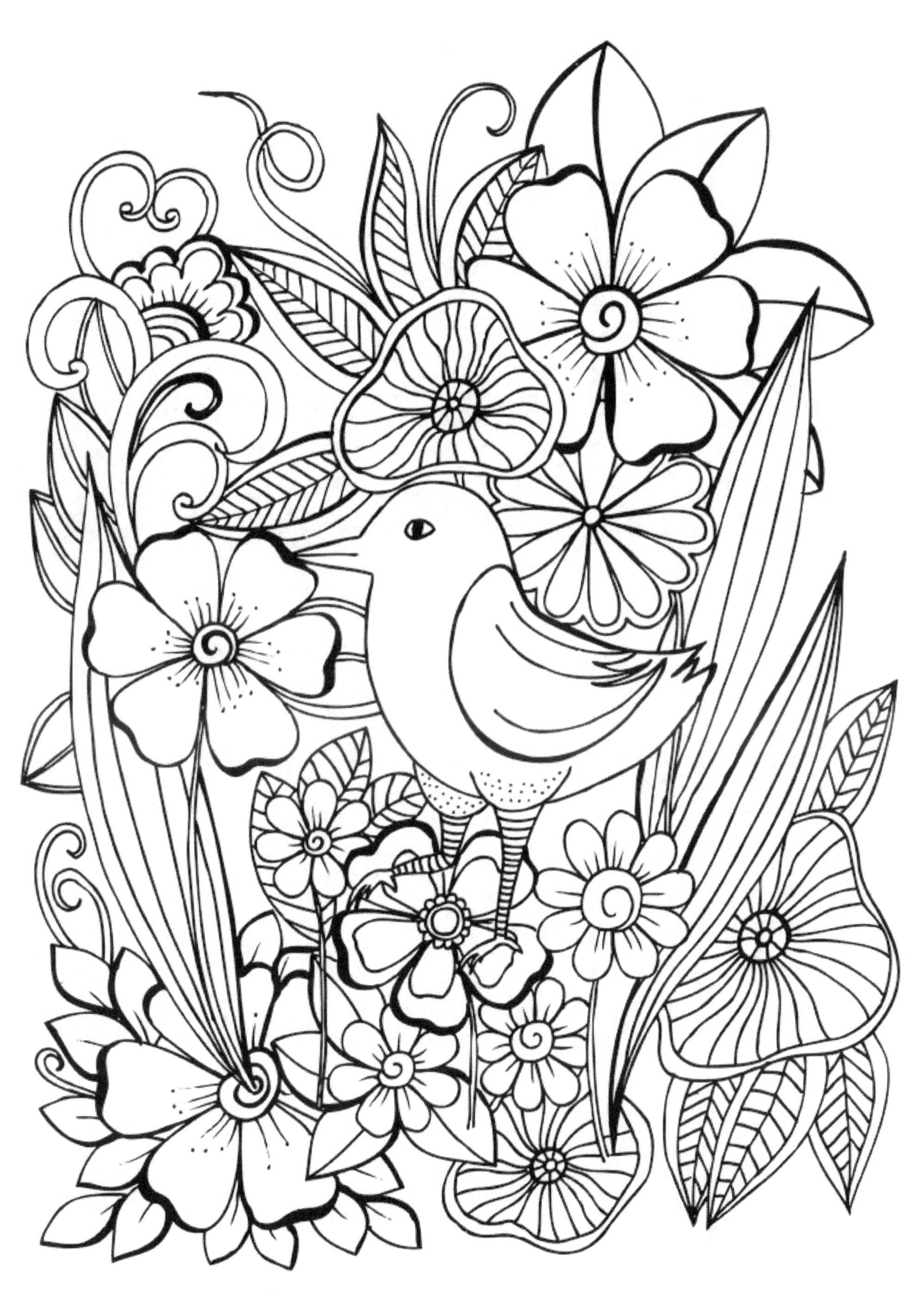

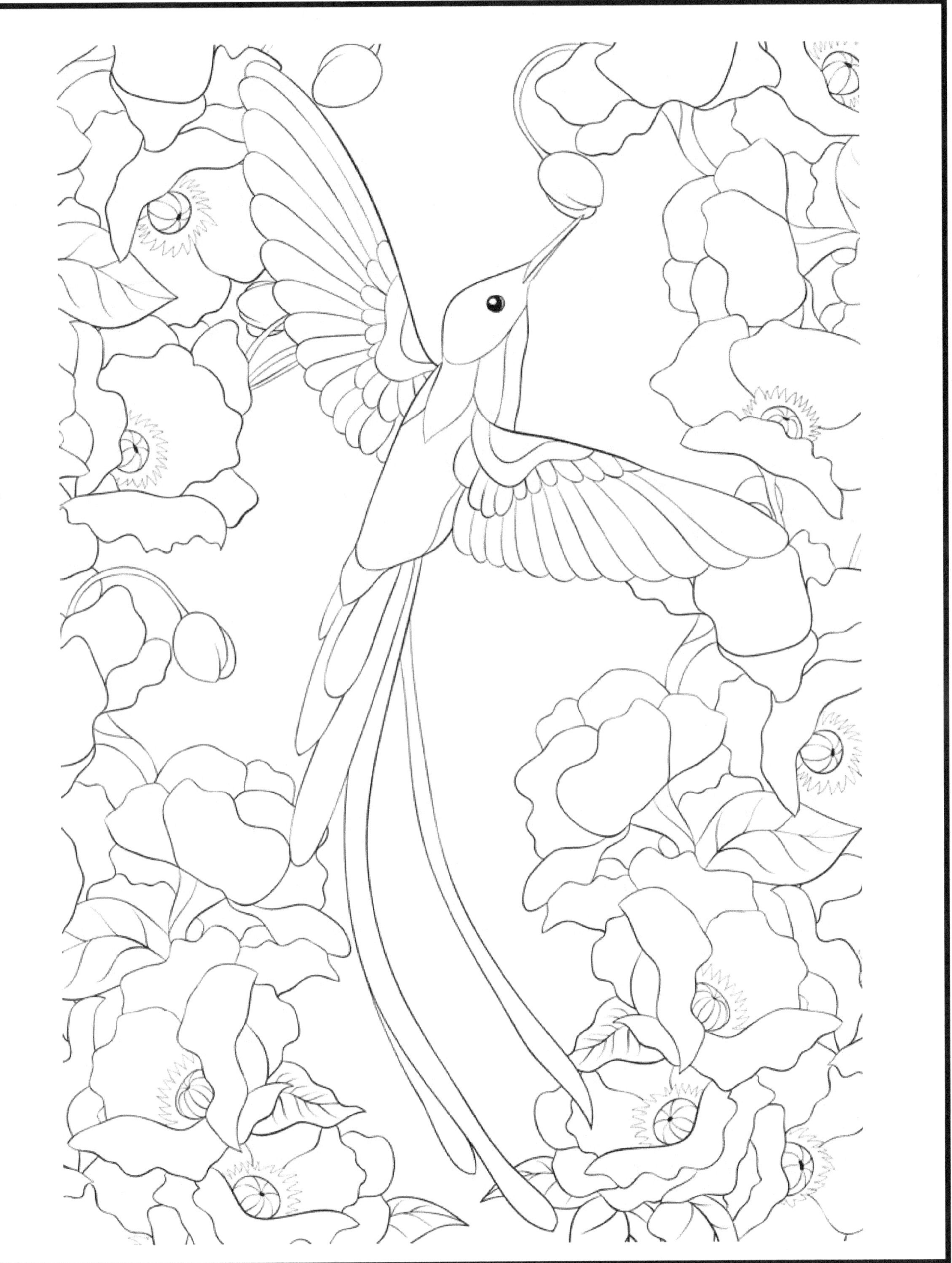

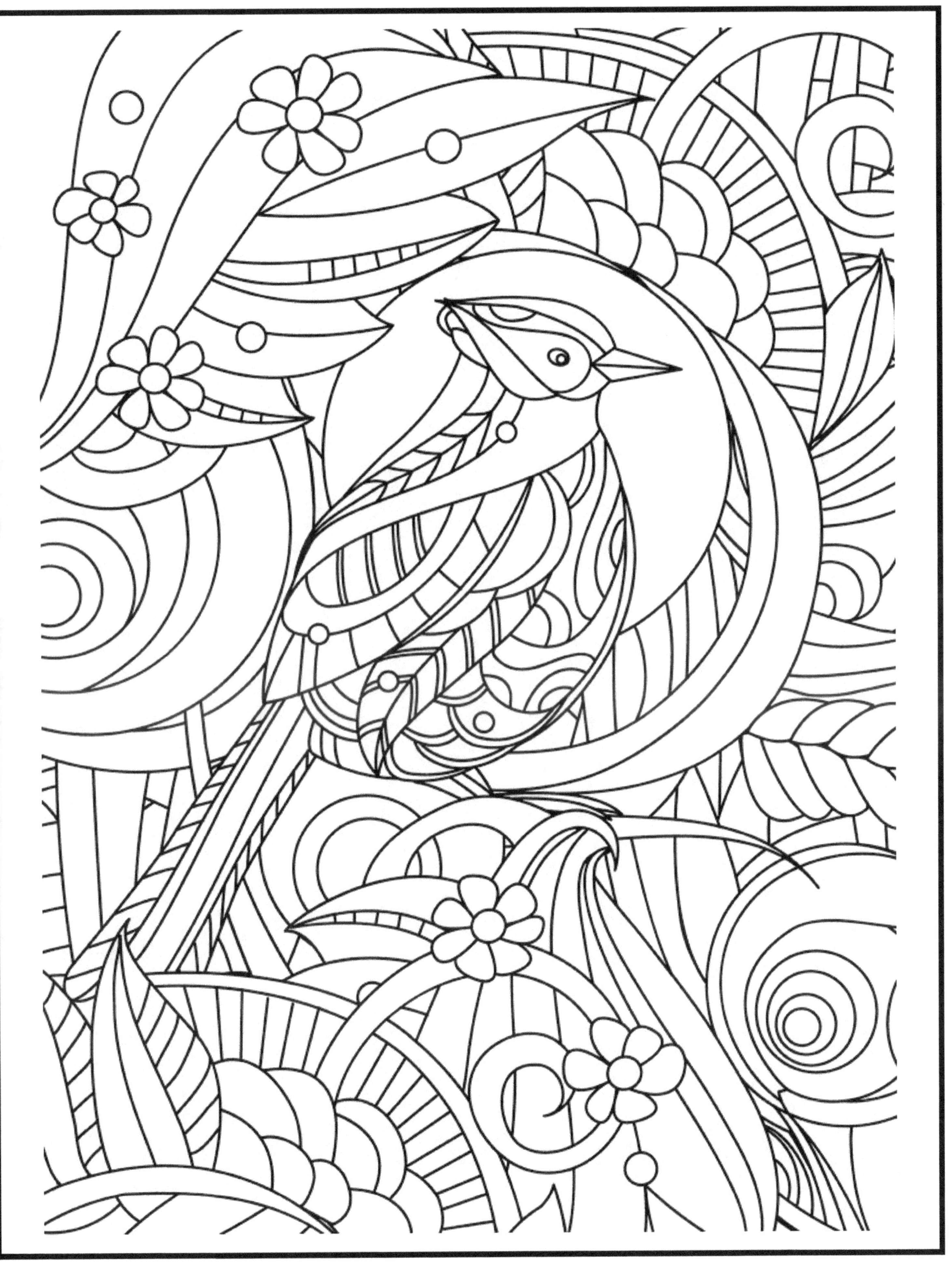

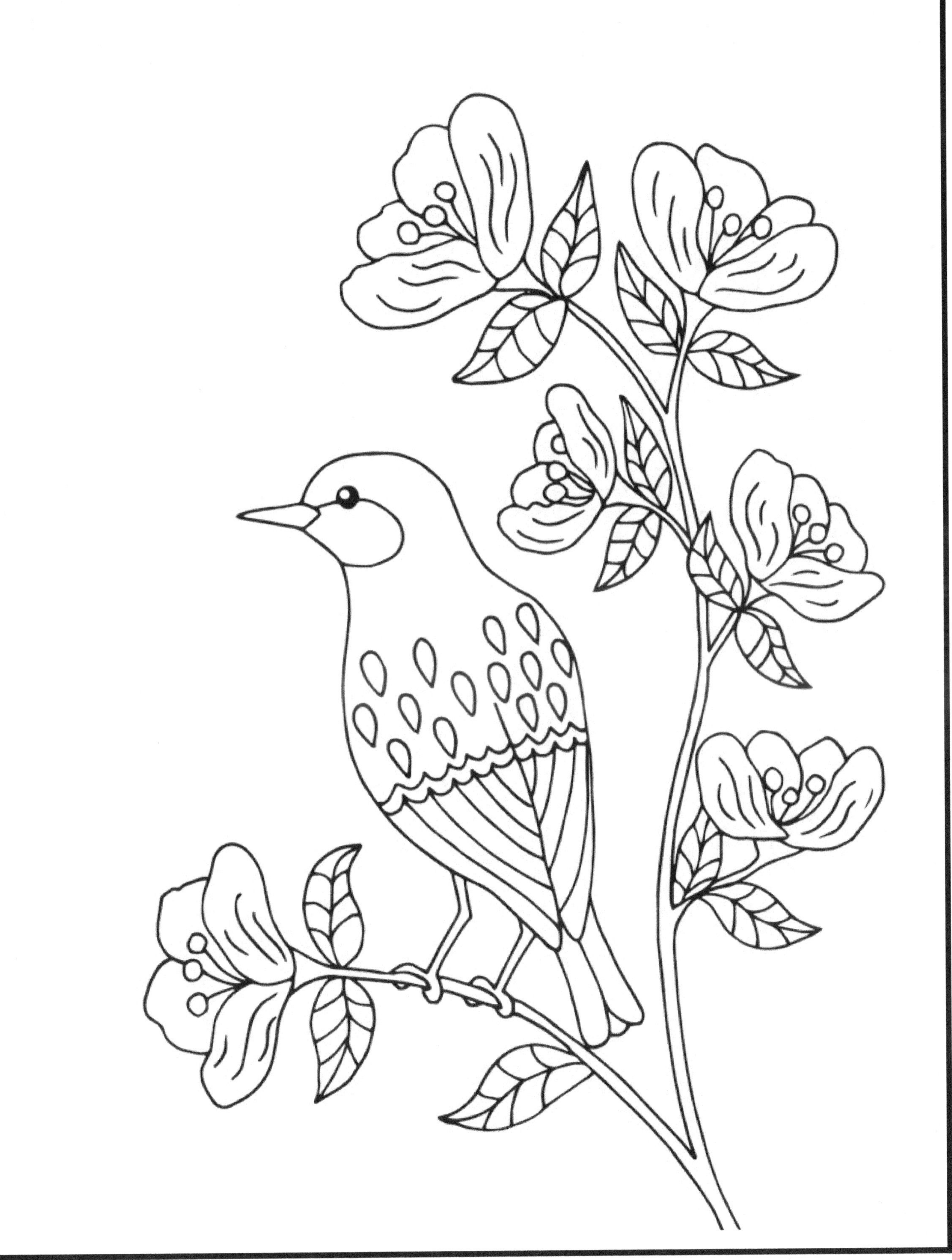

www.ingramcontent.com/pod-product-compliance
Lightning Source LLC
Chambersburg PA
CBHW080752120726
48001CB00009B/2729